To:
Terry and Jonathan,
"From the heart to the heart, may it go much further!"

Jon Huer

THE STORY OF A BOY
FAVORED BY PROVIDENCE

AUSTIN MACAULEY PUBLISHERS™

LONDON • CAMBRIDGE • NEW YORK • SHARJAH

Ordering Information
Quantity sales: Special discounts are available on quantity purchases by corporations, associations, and others. For details, contact the publisher at the address below.

Publisher's Cataloging-in-Publication data
Huer, Jon
The Story of a Boy Favored by Providence

ISBN 9781647506643 (Paperback)
ISBN 9781647506650 (ePub e-book)

Library of Congress Control Number: 2021911077

www.austinmacauley.com/us

First Published (2021)
Austin Macauley Publishers LLC
40 Wall Street, 33rd Floor, Suite 3302
New York, NY 10005
USA

mail-usa@austinmacauley.com
+1 (646) 5125767

Table of Contents

About the Book

THE STORY OF A BOY
FAVORED BY PROVIDENCE

*A Retired Professor Recalls His Childhood:
How He Survived the Korean War,
His Step-Mother, and Life as a Teenage Laborer*

A Partial Autobiography by

JON HUER
Professor Emeritus
University of Maryland

Why I am Writing My Childhood Story

By convention, memoirs are written for one of two reasons. One is that a person of recognized importance, having partaken in an important historical event, tells the story that is of public significance in recordkeeping. Winston Churchill's biography or stories of survival in the Holocaust belongs in this category, where the narrator is subsumed in the grandeur of the event itself.

The second reason for the genre of personal memoirs is in the public merits of the event, which arouses enough public curiosity or interest, such as being victims of extraordinary crimes or having been a well-known celebrity. But such memoirs are without the significance of historical dramas like Churchill's WWII or the Holocaust. The readers are interested in the details of how such events took place or personalities existed.

Often, the two categories overlap in reality, as many events are seemingly historical, such as the U.S. presidencies, which combine the larger dimensions of global power and personal gossip. On the other hand, many memoirs of no particular historical significance, such as crime stories or celebrity bios, often claim some larger importance under a 'role model' or partisan-ideological rubric. As our cultural understanding of what is historical, public interest, or private curiosity becomes increasingly harder to tell, these two reasons for writing memoirs overlap constantly.

My reason for writing this partial memoir is neither. Primarily, I am writing the story of my childhood for my son Jonathan who has never heard it before. As a typical California-bred youth, all he knows is that his father was a professor of some renown, an author who wrote many books, and that one of the books appeared in TIME magazine which praised it as 'important and often brilliant' for prophesying America's destiny as our 'national death wish.' He doesn't know anything about his father's youthful past, how he had survived the Korean War, how he had escaped from an orphanage when he was not even a teenager, how he had endured the life of a street urchin and laborer until he was nineteen, or how he became 'the most insightful of humanists' writing in America today' in spite of it all.

My wife, Terry, who has a theater background, thinks my stories are just too interesting not to tell others. I agree with her. Maybe it's worth retelling to a wider audience. What significance one may derive—biographical, moral, or historical—is up to the reader. There is nothing in the magnitude of WWII or the Holocaust in my story. But if there is any merit in simply surviving the hand that you are dealt in life with much of your own innate idealism and humanity intact, then it is an epic story of survival and worth retelling in itself.

That's why I am writing the story of my childhood.

Jon Huer
Professor Emeritus (meaning 'retired professor')
University of Maryland University College

I. In the Beginning

My story begins at the height of World War II, in what is now South Korea, then, for some odd reason, called 'The Land of the Morning Calm' by the American missionaries. But the better part of the world was hardly calm, as it was fully engaged in bloodshed in Europe as well as in the Pacific. Hitler was fighting the Soviets in an all-out war on the eastern front. The Japanese were engaged in the Pacific war against the United States. Koreans themselves, ferociously opposed to Japanese rule, fought their colonizers in every possible way they could. Some of them drifted to the Soviet Union and later became Communists to rule the north. Others migrated to the United States, then-the-citadel of freedom and liberty, and became Liberals. A third group went to China, which was in the middle of a civil war between Communists and Liberals (or 'Nationalists'), part of them later joining the North Korean Communists and part of them aligning themselves with the South Korean Liberals, depending on their individual fortunes. These Communists and Liberals, both quite new to the Koreans, determined the fate of the peninsula and its people for many decades to come. The Korean people, who had only known kings and feudal lords, and later modern colonial rulers, suddenly woke up one day and faced a new choice between two very alien ideas, Communism or Liberalism. Soviet Russia made the north a Communist nation, the 'workers' paradise;' market-society Americans made the south a Liberal nation, as in 'the world is your oyster.' As the European world waged war with Hitler, and the Japanese with Americans, with the Korean peninsula's fate hanging in the balance of the outcome, I was born.

At birth, I was given the name 'Sei-Kan,' meaning something like 'a bright light,' as all Korean babies were given Japanese names, a gift from the Japanese colonial rule in Korea. This Japanese rule, begun three decades earlier, would go on for three more years. Oblivious to the sound of groans and battle-cries elsewhere, I was born on a southernmost tropical island in South Korea called Jeju. The island is now a crowded tourist location, with hundreds of planes landing and departing every day. At the time I was born, only ships connected the paradise island and the mainland. My father, a tall, dashing tycoon of rice importation from the mainland, married my mother, second of the three daughters of a prominent family who owned one of the island's major breweries.

The wedding, from what I was later told, was a major event and I was born in the following year. In spite of all the hoopla about this celebrated couple, the real picture was somewhat darker, not as festive and bright as the celebration would have indicated. My father, the son of a wealthy silk manufacturer, had married a sixteen-year-old farm girl when he was only twelve, as was the custom then, and had run away to Japan when he was eighteen. Once in a while, this wandering husband would come home to his wife and sire children, eventually resulting in two daughters and two sons. My father kept this all a secret from my mother and her family when he started courting her. But my mother also had a story she didn't tell my father. Two years before she met my father, she had a son from her liaison with a married man. After a bitter custody fight over this son, perhaps with emphasis on 'fight' more than 'custody,' in a highly male-dominant society, she lost that son to his father. The celebrated union in paradise between a dashing rice merchant and the local beauty was already fraught with trouble. I was destined to inherit the full wrath of the sins of my father in my early life.

The baby who, three decades or so later, would be hailed as 'the most insightful of humanists writing in America today' and his analysis of America as the 'best since De Tocqueville and James Bryce' was born in Korea and speaking his first words in Japanese. From the anecdotal stories I heard years later, I was an exceedingly happy baby, talking incessantly and bubbly and adored by the adults around. But like most babies of my generation, my future was quite uncertain. Given the circumstances, that someday I would be somewhat famous in America as a professor-writer was neither foreshadowed nor likely. After all, for the moment, my present colonial master and the U.S., my future home for fame and greatness, were at war.

The earliest signs of my genius showed themselves in my prodigious talkativeness. I am not sure what other signs of genius a three-year-old baby can demonstrate other than his ability to talk and talk, and talk incessantly. (Three decades later, this talkative baby would find his calling in professional capacity as a professor at American universities.) Apparently, I was a popular baby and many relatives and friends practically fought to babysit me and play with me, enjoying their time with this adorable talking bird. A Japanese army general in command of the Japanese forces on the island and his wife were particularly fond of me, my mother told me years later, often feeding me and playing horsey with me on their laps. With the obvious signs of intelligence, even of genius, so apparent in this prodigiously talking baby, the goddess of fortune smiled on me favorably and assuredly. Japan was winning, the island was far away from the battlefront, and my father was prosperous.

When I was about three (I was later told), my parents, predominantly my father, decided to move to the large city of Gwangju, in the southern part of mainland Korea. It is likely that my mother by now knew about her husband's original wife and children and, more importantly, had reconciled with that fact. My father had lied to her, of course, but under the customs of the day, such was not considered a cardinal sin. As a businessman, my father was a great salesman who talked the talk. Presenting himself as a loyal subject of the Japanese rulers, he then succeeded in garnering all the printing businesses of the Japanese colonial government. He owned a print-shop housed in a two-story brick building which ran three shifts. Men worked day and night printing all the official documents needed for its colonial governance and my father was one of the wealthiest men in the city. He was one of those rare Korean men who affected the Japanese-style fashion heavily accented with bourgeoisie Europe. He mostly wore a tall hat and black cape with an animal-fur collar. Often smoking a pipe and wearing round horn-rimmed glasses, he favored the appearance of a well-to-do gentleman of considerable influence and means. The effect was that he looked stern and authoritative and my earliest memory of him is that I was afraid of him. In fact, townspeople held him in awe and fear. He always traveled in black rickshaws, and whenever he got out of the rickshaw with a cane in his hand, the townspeople and children who had gathered around would instantly step back with great respect. But my father was also a good politician and tactician. He gave to the townspeople generously at festivals and holidays. Often, he invited them to our house for a huge feast.

In spite of his business prosperity and town popularity, the domestic scene at our household was not a happy one. (This I was told years later, of course.) There, in the large household, was a curious mix of family conviviality and tension. The conviviality was provided by the children, several of father's original family, and now a new baby brother from the island. All of my father's children, I and my half-siblings, were wonderful in abundant peace and security. They were all older than me, the two half-sisters almost a generation older because of my father's early marriage. The tension existed largely between the two wives, my father's legal wife with her children and my mother with her precocious three-year-old. (By then, I had become my father's fifth child in the family register.) On the surface, peace and harmony prevailed in the house and the two wives lived together without outward trouble. Korea's general culture which tolerated such things, and my father's fearsome authority in the city and over the family, was too much power for the women to overcome. The two

16

women avoided challenging his authority and kept quiet with their inner feelings about this arrangement. The legal wife, whom I called 'Big Mother,' recognizing her prior status, according to the rules and customs of the day, wielded the comfort and authority of being the matriarch; my mother, who was younger and prettier, enjoyed the substance of my father's affection. The latter fact largely overcame the finer factual point that, after all, she was not my father's legitimate wife. The print-shop was humming day and night, my father was rich and powerful, and the household kept its peace.

The two-story brick building, with our large family living upstairs and the print shop occupying downstairs, still had a space left unoccupied. My father decided to rent the space out to one of his older mahjong friends who opened a photography studio there, named 'Choonwon,' meaning 'Spring Garden.' My mother, who had much free time, went to the studio, often helping the photographer and learning some rudimentary skills as a photographer herself. Of course, I was, as a cute baby of three or so, the favorite subject of her camera and as a result, hundreds of pictures were taken of me by the doting photographer apprentice. Some of my early studio photos show a well-fed, bright child who, unlike most children in the poor, colonized country, wore fashionable and expensive clothes that were popular in metropolitan Tokyo. Except for the few that survived, most of my childhood photos were destroyed during the Korean War, as was the family that kept them for my mother. Of course, nobody could foresee that the 'Spring Garden Studio,' an unassuming small portrait studio in Gwuangju, would play a crucial role almost two decades later in the life of such a bubbly, bright baby when things got really desperate for him.

Beneath the harmonious and peaceful surface, however, the tension between the two strong-willed women (Korean women are nothing if they are not strong-willed.) was becoming palpable. Two events, one international and the other domestic, took place to break the routine surface harmony and peace. Internationally, World War II came to an end as Japan surrendered and withdrew from Korea. With that, my father's prosperity, doing all the printing business for the ruling Japanese, came to an abrupt end. Domestically, my father, apparently not satisfied with the two wives, engaged another woman, still younger and prettier than my mother, as his concubine, a contract wife. My Big Mother, accustomed to her husband's wayward behavior for many years, endured this new development in silent obstinacy. But my mother, who had grown up as one of the three rather well-bred, spirited girls on the island in a proud family, could not tolerate her husband's new woman. In an ironic way, my father had left his first farm-girl of a wife for a younger and more attractive woman, i.e., my mother. But my father now preferred another woman who was much younger and more attractive than my mother. In the normal turn of life, my mother had it coming. But unlike my father's old farm-girl of a wife who was largely silent, my mother was furious. In great anger and indignation, she stalked her husband to the concubine's house unobserved and made a public scene. Thereafter, more scenes of public argument followed, and my parents' union came to a breaking point. The concubine culture, a man taking a younger woman as a contract wife, assumes that his present wife accepts this arrangement, at least tacitly. When this silent agreement is not possible, something has to happen. Either the union breaks up, which is rare, or the husband gives up the new concubine partner, which is rarer. My mother was neither, and was in a rather tenuous position with her husband. Upset and sorrowful, she returned to the island several times to consult her older sister. After all, her older sister's husband was the mayor of the second largest city on the island and carried some influence, as his family was reputed to 'own half the island.'

My mother, when she made another hurried trip to the island after one of the scenes with my father, made a terrible tactical mistake; she returned to the island that time without me, hardly thinking that this would be the last time she would see her baby. Many years later, I asked her why she had left me with father instead of taking me with her, as it turned out to be the most pivotal event in my entire life. Her answer was that my father had promised her that she would be allowed to take the baby back when she returned to the household. She should have known that my father was a good salesman, quite capable of a sweet-talk deception. When she came back to the household in Gwangju to take me, as she was planning to leave her husband, her treacherous husband had changed his mind. He would not allow her or any of her relatives to take the boy. My mother, on her part, had anticipated trouble and also came with enforcement in the form of several male relatives. A serious family feud over Sei-Kan, now three going on four, was about to begin. My father, on his part, had some of the off-duty print-shop workers surround me so that I could not be taken physically by my mother's men. By then, her older

19

sister had joined the group to lend moral and tactical support. For many days, the tussle between the two groups, the islanders and the mainlanders, went on, attacking and defending over the fate of a very talkative genius. Naturally, I had no idea this was going on, and even now, I have no idea how my life would have been lived differently depending on whose side won.

At that time in Korea, now that the ruling Japanese authority had hurriedly withdrawn from their colony, the formal law was no use in the ensuing social chaos. There was neither a reliable legal system nor an effective police force in the city. The American military set up a temporary government to administer this ex-colony of Japan, but it was woefully unreliable and ineffective. In this vacuum of government and law, the two opposing groups of men, under the command of my mother and my father, respectively, fought to take the boy. It was strictly a family affair, over which the law was neither available nor asked to intervene. Although the world was finally at peace after the horrific war in Europe and in the Pacific, my parents continued their own war over their little son.

Eventually, the internecine war between my parents ended with Father's victory. The locals won. My mother's forces finally recognized that they could not win the battle and decided to return to the island defeated and empty-handed. My mother, from what I heard later, wailed in the streets for her son and left the city in great sorrow and grief. For the second time in her young life, she lost her son to another dominant man. Both of her sons were now in the custody of their fathers, yanked out of her arms in their tender early years. Life in my father's household now returned to normal. But this normal life was broken up one day, not too long after my parental battle had ended, when nobody could find me. I had disappeared! My father sent his workers all over the city to find me. By evening, they finally found me at the train station, close to a mile from home. Astonished, they inquired what I was doing at the train station. According to the legend that had grown around this incident, I said to the astonished men, "I want my mommy." I told the men that I had come to the station to ride the train to see my mother.

In the ensuing days and months, what I had remembered about my mother faded, and in time I forgot all about her. After all, I had two mothers who doted over me, my Big Mother and the new concubine mother who joined the household in place of my mother. Soon, I began to call the new concubine mother 'New Mom,' and eventually just 'Mom' upon her request. I still called my father's legal wife 'Big Mother,' whose title indicated her matriarchal status and the fact that she was above all other women in the hierarchy of my father's fiefdom.

When I was about five, my father decided to close the print-shop, which was declining since the Japanese withdrawal, and go into a fishing business. From printing to fishing was a rather radical entrepreneurial change, but father was uncanny with his business acumen. Father decided upon yellow croaker ('goolbi' in Korean), which was becoming quite popular in Korea. The yellow croaker was, as still is, a smelly but delicious fish which had become the most honored fish as chosen to be served on the banquet table of the ancestors on their death anniversaries. Because it was caught only in the limited southwestern sea, it was, and still is, quite expensive. Even today, Koreans who wish to show respects or bribe somebody choose the half-dry yellow croakers as a desirable present. My father had a good sense of where the next gold mine was, and chose the yellow croaker as his next business.

He bought a fishing boat, quite large by the prevailing standards, in partnership with another man and moved to a small fishing village about a hundred miles southwest of Gwangju. The family that he decided to take to the fishing village with him included me and the concubine mother. Also included in our new family unit was a young teenage girl, whose name I cannot remember (Koreans prefer to use relational titles, such as 'uncle' or 'cousin,' rather than names.), who my father and his concubine wife had informally adopted as their daughter. We settled in a small fishing village called 'Mong-neng-gi,' a rather odd name even in Korean, and lived there for the next three years.

With her pretty face and sophisticated demeanor, my concubine mother was quite different from my stoic Big Mother who came from a farming family. Concubines in Korea had their origins in Japan's geisha group who entertained men with arts and performances. When their performing days were over as they got older, their next career move was in attaching themselves to rich old men to become their second wives, the 'concubine.' My New Mother, although she originated from a farming family herself, had been a geisha in her younger years. Keenly aware of their status as non-legal wives, they served their men on contract and retired from work when their contract husband either died of old age or returned to their original wives to die.

My father's keen sense of business opportunities served him well with the fish. He was once again a rich town leader in Mong-neng-gi, which was one of the ports closest to the spot in the sea where the yellow croaker was abundant. He bought a two-story house near the beach at the corner of the main street, where a Japanese merchant had once lived. It was only about a block or so from the water. My earliest memories began here and life was great. At night, children of my age congregated at the street in front of our house, where my father officiated our Korean-style wrestling matches. Winners were rewarded with food and money, and this nightly event was always popular. As the healthy and well-fed child of the richest man in town, I won many of the matches which were held under the dangling bare light bulb at the front of the house. These are some of the earliest memories of my childhood, and very happy ones. I remember virtually nothing of my life at the print-shop house in Gwangju, and I gathered the experiences of my life there only through the stories my family later told me. Thus, all the battles and wars between my father's men and my mother's relatives over me, thanks to no memory, left no emotional scars. But my early life in Mong-neng-gi remains quite vivid to this day.

My earliest memory consists entirely of Mong-neng-gi, which was a small fishing village. I remember that there were two large dirt roads that crossed each other in front of our house, located on the corner toward the beach. The road that ran by our house down the hill toward the beach passed between two rows of mud houses and thatched roofs where fishermen and farmers lived. In contrast to these humble mud houses, ours was a conspicuously large two-story wooden structure. The small half-moon-shaped beach at the end of the road served as the village's little harbor that my father's fishing boat called home. Standing on the breakwater of the beach, you could see several uninhabited rock-islets through which the fishing boats left the port and came home. The other dirt road that crossed in front of my house went a block or so to meet the highway that led to the larger nearby town where the schools were located. If you followed this road in the opposite direction, it would lead to two or three tiny fishing villages that, along with Mong-neng-gi, dotted the coast. A small mountain on one side and the open fields, rice paddies and dry fields, planted and harvested in different seasons, on the other, encompassed our little village's landscape. Our village was small and it was peaceful. (Fifty or so years later, I and my wife revisited the place, but even the local police could not identify where exactly Mong-neng-gi was or had been. My wife, uncannily good with geographic intuition, was very certain that the small nuclear power plant we saw had been built where Mong-neng-gi used to be. If true, the fifty-year span between my life there and the nuclear power plant embodies the entire history of modern Korea.)

Peace and quiet, yes, but actually, the town was bustling with activities when my family arrived there. In fact, all of Korea, just liberated from Japanese rule, was bustling with nation-building businesses. After thirty-six years of colonial rule under Japan, which kept Korea rather undeveloped and pre-modern, Koreans had much catching up to do. I remember lining up at a schoolyard with other kids, with our sleeves rolled up to get small pox vaccines. A policeman on horseback came to our town to introduce himself as the new lawman. My adopted sister, a teenager who had never attended school before, now had to learn how to read and write. My parents (The concubine mother had assumed the role of my regular mother by then.) had hired a tutor from the nearby town to teach her the Korean alphabet, which had been forbidden during Japanese colonial rule. The tutor brought with him a wall poster that listed the vowels and consonants that formed Korea's written words. He used the poster as a device to teach the teenage girl how to read and write for the first time in her life. The academic progress seemed slow.

For my part, I was now a precocious six-year-old in a bustling household with many men and women working around the clock, and I was quite popular. Whenever Father had visitors, he called me indoors and would tell me to 'sing for our guests.' I would stand straight up and sing a few tunes, which always ended with handclapping and praise. Then, I would return outside to play.

One of the things going on in the household that drew my special attention was my aforementioned sister's learning. Up to that time, I too had never been engaged in any organized intellectual activities that involved learning and was naturally drawn by curiosity to what she was doing. Apparently not born with my genius streak, she was having a tough time memorizing the twenty-seven vowels and consonants, and a tougher time combining these letters to form words and sentences. Once every so often, drawn by my curiosity, I would sneak into the room and watch the struggle my adopted sister and her tutor were having. One day, their struggle was particularly pronounced as I heard the tutor's voice rising higher than usual at my sister's

25

inability to form words and sentences. It must have been her exam day, as my parents and a couple of household workers were there to witness the results of their considerable labor and expense. As I walked into the room, the disappointment was palpable. I saw my adopted sister's head dropped and the tutor's eyebrows rose. I instantly recognized the task in front of her, which she had obviously failed.

"I know how to do that," I said innocently. The whole room turned to me in astonishment, all of them mouthing the word, "What?"

I repeated my announcement. After a silent surprise, my father turned to me and said, "You mean you know to read and write?"

I said, still very innocently, "Yes, I know how to read and write."

There was some more silence at the audacity of this little boy who had never been taught reading and writing. Finally, the roomful of adults were convinced that it was not a silly boasting of a child. My father urged the equally astonished tutor to give me the task with which my adopted sister was struggling. I sat at the table and, taking the pencil and paper in front of me, wrote down the sentence the tutor had dictated. (Actually I misspelled one letter.) My memory fails me at this point, for I don't remember the logical eruption of the adults in the room that must have been considerable. They were witnessing a six-year-old who had never been taught to read or write demonstrating the fluency of reading and writing. Although I remember nothing of their reaction, they must have had the same thought, *This boy is a genius!* Indeed, several months later I started going to the local elementary school and, to the teacher's surprise,

I knew how to read and write, being the only first grader who could do that. Well, the competition was rather weak at this point, as the boys in my grade were all children of poor farmers and fishermen who spent most of their time helping their parents with work, not exploring their intellectual curiosity. I was the local wrestling champion and the only first-grader who knew how to read and write, not to mention being the only son of the richest man in this quiet fishing village. I could not be happier.

My father's fishing business was thriving with the abundance of the yellow croaker. The ship usually stayed at sea for about a week while it was hauling in the fish. There was always a huge festival, with a lot of drinking and dancing and eating, whenever the fishing vessel went to the sea and again when it returned home after a shipload of the catch. With much drinking and shouting, the whole village came out to enjoy the festivity. I remember one night (It must have been the vessel's return.) when one villager, a man, had ingested the toxic intestines of a blow fish, which could be fatal. With no doctors or hospitals in the village, the man was struggling to stay awake, for sleep was fatal. The townspeople took turns to keep him awake and walking all night, holding him up from both sides. I remember the noise and bustle of festivity mixed with the urgent business of lifesaving all through the night. (I don't remember if the man eventually survived.) Once in a while, the vessel was sent to the nearest port city for regular repair and supply and I was often invited to sail with the crew. I remember the crew amusing me on the ship and watching the vast deep blue sea waving by. Once at the port, the fishermen would take me to the candy shops where all sorts of sweets were being spun on their little taffy machines. I usually came home with bags of candy, which I shared with the village boys.

Our household was always full of men and women who worked for my parents. Women worked downstairs, cooking and cleaning the rooms, as my father had numerous guests and visitors. Men worked mostly for my father's fishing business, drying and shipping the yellow croakers all year round. Once in a while, several of my father's men would go to the mountain nearby to collect dead trees for firewood and they would take me with them. They were quite raucous with their dirty jokes, generally involving their imagined carnal relations with my adopted sister, and would laugh uproariously at their own jokes. Their jokes were particularly delightful to them because they could tell the jokes in front of the girl's brother who had no idea what they were talking about. My ignorance of what they were saying added more strength to their guffaw.

They were always good to me and I had a lot of fun with them whenever they took me on their trips to the mountain. The men sang and laughed a great deal among themselves. Often, they found delicious berries and fruits in the mountain and shared them with me. The days were warm and life seemed sweet and innocent, and these men were my guardians and protectors. One time, I came down with chickenpox and was bedridden for a few days. The family kept me in the attic, far away from the rest of the household. The men came by and entertained me with a bat that they had captured, now on a string. They tied the bat to one of the beams in the attic and amused me and themselves greatly as the bat flapped around in the room.

When school started, the kids in our village gathered and walked through the fields to our school in the next town. Although a good dirt road from my house to the next town existed, the kids and I ended up going through the fields as a 'shortcut.' We enjoyed the irregularities of going through the fields, hopping over holes with snakes and fertilizer, instead of the safe but monotonous dirt road. On school days, my father always kept me dressed in the best of clothes and equipped with the newest items for school and play. He bought the most expensive leather book-bag for me, and it instantly became the object of envy among the poor kids. I intensely disliked being the only kid with such a shiny object causing such envy from the other kids. Sometimes when the weather was not good, with rain or sleet or even threat of it, my father had one of his men carry me piggyback to school. Kids would laugh, pointing at me riding on the man's back, and, so embarrassed and ashamed, I would struggle to get down.

The fields, when no crops were planted or growing, mostly had that sweet smell of earth and air. But sometimes, especially in the spring, the fields had other smells as well. At that time in Korea, human feces was still the most common and effective form of fertilizer, especially when aged in a hole dug in the corner of a field. Farmers collected feces from the outhouses and stored them in the 'honey pots,' as they were euphemistically called. This accounted for the smell other than that of sweet earth and air. These honey pots varied in size, some large and some small, depending on the size of the field. The kids on the way to school were careful to avoid these honey pots, as the large kids threatened to push the little ones into these holes, normally causing an uproar among us. When spring came, the farmers used the now-aged feces in honey pots to fertilize their fields.

On one lunar New Year's Day, I was out playing with the village boys, most of them older than me. Lunar New Year's Day, the most celebrated holiday in Asian nations, generally comes in February, quite cold and often snowy. My father had ordered the best-quality new clothes from the city for me to wear for the festive holiday. Included in the new clothes was a beautiful wool sweater the village kids could only fantasize wearing. Still, other kids wore their own best clothes for the holiday, and we were enjoying the holiday festivity all around us. Like a flock of birds flying here and there without direction, we ran around in the village, laughing breathless and silly, greeting the elders whenever we met them and getting money for each bow. Then we all ran to the beach to play in the deserted fishing boat left in the sand. That New Year's Day was windy and cold, and the wind started rocking the boat on which we were playing. As the wind got heavier, the boat swayed as if it were going to turn over. The boys, mostly bigger than me, jumped off the boat and started running toward the dry field. I followed them as usual, trying to keep pace with the older kids, mostly shouting and jumping and in the mood for the holiday. We were running and hopping in the field when we came to one of the honey pots full of aging fertilizer. The boys hesitated as they got close to the honey pot and looked at the fertilizer pool with some serious decision-making. But it was a holiday, and the wild wind and the energy from all the running and shouting had brought the boys up to a level of daring somewhat beyond their normal prudence. The result was that they decided to jump over the honey pot. They backed away from the pot and, getting a sufficient running start, jumped over the fertilizer storage pool. Since the honey pot in question was a medium-sized pool, they jumped over it easily. My turn came and, naturally imitating the older kids, I jumped over the fertilizer pot from the running start and safely landed on the other side. The older kids ran on for a few more steps as if they were going to continue to run in a new direction. Emboldened by their first success, however, the boys became bolder and then walked around the pool and came to the spot from which they had made their first jump. There, they repeated their earlier success and jumped over the honey pot, once again all of them landing safely on the other side. With the same instinct as before, I followed the older boys and jumped over the fertilizer pool after the older kids. Except that this time, I was not successful in landing safely on the other side. I fell straight into the fertilizer pool filled with well-fermented human feces getting ready for the field in the spring. Shocked, the boys pulled me up from the hole, which filled up close to my chest. Seeing me, now dripping with the human fertilizer all over my fine clothes, the boys scattered away.

One could accurately say I cried all the way home, perhaps a couple of blocks from the scene of the accident. My father, who was in bed with a severe cold, was not happy to see me coming home crying and dripping with the fermented human fertilizer. It so happened that, because it was New Year's Day, all the helpers had gone to their hometowns which included the concubine mother, and Father was the only person in the house. He struggled to get out of bed and, with great effort, succeeded. The sight of me was too miserable and polluted to wash me down in the house. I was just too filthy for in-house washing. My father decided to take me to the beach, about a hundred yards or so away. The father and son trudged down the narrow path to the beach, some neighbors watching us curiously and laughing when they realized what was going on. We finally reached the water in the wind and the cold. There, my father stripped me of my clothes, including that beautiful wool sweater, and hurled the soiled clothes into the ocean. Of course, I never saw them again. My father used the sea water to wash me and brought me back home.

In spite of this memorable incident, the three years we lived in Mong-neng-gi was full of happiness and comfort. I was at the center of attention most of the time, as my father was wealthy and I was on the verge of being considered a genius. Not in inconsiderate part for my popularity was the attraction my adopted sister held to the men who worked for my father. But this was *my* paradise, not my half-brothers' or half-sisters' and certainly not their mother's who was left in Gwangju. They lived in a nice house and were well provided for by my father who kept them abundantly supplied and comfortably financed. But they had never been part of my father's love or attention. My Big Mother was perhaps the most miserable woman in the city, whose rich husband lived somewhere else with his favorite son and an attractive consort. She managed to send one of her sons, two years older than me, but much bigger and taller than the two years would indicate, to Mong-neng-gi to be with his father during the summers. One summer, while we were roughhousing, I accidentally pushed him down the stairs, which skinned his shin badly, exposing the bone. This did not heal for a while and he took every chance thereafter to accuse me of pushing him deliberately. Aside from this pushdown incident, I don't remember anything about how we, my half-brother and I, played together as if we had never been together in the fishing village. The two half-brothers of mine, both tall, strong, and athletic, were not academically inclined. (Both of them became successful boxers, good enough to try out for the Olympics to represent Korea.) But contrary to these older sons, I was practically a genius, scoring a perfect hundred on virtually every exam. This disparity in our intellectual developments added more bitterness to the miserable woman who was scorned and left to her loneliness in another city. Once, it was my own mother who had taken over the affection of her rightful husband. Now it was my concubine mother, both younger and prettier, who was monopolizing the pleasure of being the matriarch of my father's affection and wealth. The full extent of her bitterness would rain down on me one day like a great storm. But for the time being, I was a happy child, still shy with an egalitarian temperament but without a care in the world.

When I was beginning second grade, Father's wanderlust hit him again and he decided to move back to Gwangju. He sold his fishing business to his partner who had a sweet daughter about my age. The day we left Mong-neng-gi, it was late afternoon. The girl shyly gave me a little something wrapped in newspaper. I opened it and found a baked sweet potato, still warm and smelling nice. A truck came and loaded all the household goods that had not been shipped earlier. Considering the great position my father

33

had occupied for the previous three years in the village, there was no fanfare about our departure. I don't remember anybody saying goodbye to us as our truck left the intersection in front of our house. During the several hours of the trip back to the city, I ate the girl's parting gift and slept.

When we arrived in Gwangju, Father had us settle in my Big Mother's household. I cannot remember whether my concubine mother had stayed with us, but my guess is that she had discretely and tactfully stayed out of sight while we were in transition. In spite of the leg injury I had caused him, my half-brother was extremely nice to me, showing me all the good-quality Japanese-made marbles and other toys he had, and we played together. My Big Mother, on her part, was very sweet to me while we had a joint household with her.

Soon after we had returned to Gwangju, Father took me to the local elementary school where I was enrolled to join its second-grade class in progress. On the first day of school, I came home on my own without waiting for someone to come and pick me up. It was a new city, the capital of the province and quite large, and it was my first day of school and they assumed I would not know how to get back home on my own. They were astounded that I navigated home alone, and this episode added another chapter to my legend as a boy genius.

My father resumed playing mahjong with his old partners in the city. One partner he visited often to play mahjong with was the doctor whose hospital shared a fence with our house. Father made a small opening in the fence so that he could take a shortcut to the hospital to play mahjong with the doctor when he was between patients. Often, I accompanied my father to the hospital, a cavernous building in which a section was occupied by the doctor's family. Once in a while, a pretty young woman, apparently the doctor's daughter, came out and watched the adults play mahjong and a small boy who was sitting next to one of the adults.

My father did not stay with his legal wife and her family very long. He found a house on the other side of the city and announced that he was moving out to live in the new home. Of course, his new household would have his favorite son and concubine wife. His legal first wife and her children would have no part in it. Once again, my unhappy Big Mother and her children had to endure the bitterness of their husband and father moving out into a separate household— without them.

The house my father chose was nice, overlooking the city's largest river, which by then had only a small stream of water running in it. The water was dammed up to help the women who washed their laundry. I learned to swim in the dammed reservoir while playing in the water with our neighborhood kids. The road in front of the house ran about three blocks or so to City Hall, a huge imposing redbrick building which was clearly visible from our house. Moving into the new part of the city, life went on uneventfully for me.

II. The War Breaks out

Another year passed and I was in third grade when the rumors of war reverberated throughout the Korean peninsula. Korea had been divided into North Korea and South Korea at the end of WWII when Japan surrendered and withdrew from the peninsula. The northern half was occupied by the Soviet-backed Communists and the southern half by the America-backed market-society Liberals. In fact, the north was governed by the Communist Party, and the south by the Syngman Rhee-controlled Liberal Party, facing each other as ideological enemies. (Ironically, Karl Marx, the founder of Communism, and Thomas Jefferson, the articulator of Liberalism, believed in the same thing, that is, equality and freedom for all). Between 1945 and 1947, South Korea was ruled by the U.S. military which filled the vacuum of government left by the sudden withdrawal of the Japanese colonial rulers. The south, with little or no industrial infrastructure, had to rely on the north for the supply of electric power. The north, on the other hand, was weak in food production and the south supplied its northern brethren with the agricultural products. This uneasy coexistence lasted several years during which the north refused to participate in the south's elections, preferring to go alone as a separate country. There was preparation going on in the north to unify both halves militarily into one nation. The south, relying on the U.S. for protection, was hardly ready for an all-out war with the north. In the meantime, the south was wrecked with daily agitations by the Communists backed by the north and the Soviets. Soon, the U.S. withdrew its main forces to Japan, leaving South Korea as a tempting target for the Communists.

My part in this conflict consisted of observing that electric power, supplied by the north, started getting shorter and more irregular. We were also told to tape the windows to prevent shattering in case of bombs. Through these uneasy signs, my life still consisted mainly of going to school and coming home in relative tranquility. Then on June 25, 1950, a Sunday, the North Korean Army attacked South Korea massively on all fronts across the famed Thirty-Eighth Parallel which had divided the two. The two militaries, Korean and American (which hurriedly brought its main forces back from Japan), got caught totally unprepared and lost the capital city of Seoul in no time. The superior North Korean Army was sweeping through the south, ultimately galloping toward Pusan, the southeastern tip of Korea, for full occupation of the peninsula.

All throughout this war development, my life was hardly affected, other than drawing more war-related pictures of tanks and bombers during our art class. Gwangju, although one of the largest cities in the south, never saw a real battle. The South Korean Military and its American allies hurriedly left the city when the North Koreans had advanced close enough. Each household had been told to dig a shelter under the house. Father decided that our house, just by the river, had no need for a shelter. He said we could dash out into the large drainage pipe, almost always dry, that started from the city and opened into the river. The pipe was large enough to accommodate many adults. We would all crawl into the pipe, wait out the raid which no one seemed to really fear, and go back to the house when it was all clear. Father got tired of this ritual and eventually decided to dig a shelter under the house. The school was finally closed and I helped the men with the digging of the shelter, which was more fun than going to school and drawing battle scenes we had never seen.

As war was raging somewhere, the wise heads, and hearts, decided that children should be evacuated to the countryside. By then, my oldest half-brother, a few years older than my other half-brother, had joined the army. My half-sister, almost a generation older than me, had left the city long before the Communists came because her husband was a policeman, a good target for Communist reprisal. So my remaining half-brother and I were the candidates for evacuation.

My concubine mother had in the meantime become my 'mother,' no longer called 'New Mother' by me. Now recognized as my *bona fide* mother, she attended PTA meetings and field-day events, and, in other ways, acted as my real mother. She came from a farming family not too far from the city, and Father decided to send his two boys to her family in the country for safety. Her family of farmers, kind and honest people, welcomed the two boys who were packed and sent to their rural village. Since there was neither a vehicle nor gasoline available, Father had arranged an ox-driven cart with all our belongings and supplies loaded for the trip to the farm house in the country. My concubine mother's family, who had obviously been helped by my father's financial largesse, was happy to see the two boys from the city.

I had visited the farm family before with my concubine mother, perhaps for a wedding or maybe a funeral. I don't remember what event had prompted our visit, but I vividly, and embarrassingly, remembered the episode of bedwetting the whole time we were there, likely three nights in a row. The strange setting must have upset my delicate night schedule. I remembered how nice the family was to me, as they good-humoredly changed the bedding night after night.

This time, neither a wedding nor a funeral but war prompted our stay. The family put us in a room with old grandma. She was completely senile, with long gray hair and thin silent smiles she flashed whenever she saw us. There was a stream of refugees coming down south, from somewhere north, maybe the capital, that passed by the farm house located on a fairly large dirt road. My concubine mother's family prepared a huge cauldron of soup for the haggard refugees and gave them encouraging words while offering them bowls of their soup. The refugees ate the soup hurriedly, thanked them, and continued their journey south. This stream of refugees, with belongings on their backs and heads, desperate and tired, was one of the few scenes I could remember of the war. While we were staying at the farmhouse, the area changed its government and the North Korean Army occupied the village. The situation changed radically for us with the new ruler in power. All the boys were rounded up for Communist education. We were taught

Communist songs, starting with the North Korean national anthem which profusely praised its leader, Kim ll Sung. The boys also marched in columns, calling out cadences loudly and singing the new songs they had learned. Then came the marching drills and bamboo-stick bayonet practices, whereby the boys were taught to poke straw objects with their sharp bamboo sticks. I was not terribly interested in the bayonet drills and they eventually excused me for being a weak boy from the city.

One early morning when it was still dark outside, my half-brother nudged me awake and pointed to something. It was the senile grandma, our roomie. She cut a ghostly figure under the small oil lamp, folding and unfolding a piece of cloth with her hands, her long gray hair covering much of her face. It was utterly quiet outside and only her own tiny rustling movement could be heard. It was a scary scene. "She is a spirit-ghost," my half-brother whispered. Although he was a big boy for his age, now he looked pale and terrified. "We'd better get out of here. She is gonna kill us with a curse!"

Of course, there was no logical reason to be scared of this old senile woman, but at the moment, what my half-brother suggested made perfect sense. Although my half-brother was only two years older than me, his bigger height and stature as an athlete at school gave him great authority over me. In fact, I was always afraid of him. I quickly obeyed him and, gathering our few belongings, we quietly crept out of the room, and eventually the house. The streams of refugees had stopped some time ago and there was hardly any human being on the road back to the city. We backtracked our ox-driven roads and eventually reached the city late that afternoon. My half-brother, not being part of my father's household, parted company with me and went back to his mother's home. I trudged back to my parents by the river. They were quite surprised to see me back from the countryside safe-house. I told them I didn't want to go back there again and they accepted my explanation and asked no further questions.

The next day, I developed a terrible pain on my right leg where the thigh joined the hip. There was a visible swelling at the joint. Father took me to the doctor's office on the next block, one of his mahjong buddies, only a couple of houses from ours. Our household always had some young men working for my father's business, mostly wheeling and dealing in wholesale, and several women who worked in domestic capacity for my concubine mother. Just like Mong-neng-gi, our house in Gwangju had much traffic, with men and women coming and going. But they mostly stayed away from the two-room section of our L-shaped house, one for me and one for my parents, so that we did not always run into each other.

One of the men accompanied by father piggybacked me to the doctor's office. But the scene that greeted us was quite surprising. The doctor's office had been turned into a military hospital for the North Korean Army. The building, an old Japanese-built structure with many wooden walls and windows, not common for Korea, was filled with wounded soldiers at various stages of recovery. The only thing I didn't see was the scenes of freshly wounded soldiers being brought in, simply because there were no frontline battles nearby. Obviously, battles were fought in some faraway places and this hospital served as the rear-line facility for recovery and recuperation. I had walked by the building often before, but never knew that such activities were going on inside. Perhaps the traffic was being handled on the backside of the hospital and we couldn't see it from the front road. My father's mahjong-buddy doctor was still there to greet us. He had me X-rayed and told my father something like the long walk from the farmhouse had enlarged and infected my lymph node in the joint, which required a small operation. Since it was late in the day, the operation was scheduled for the next day. Upon this decision, my father's man piggybacked me back home.

Of course, at the time I was too young to realize all this medical stuff, but understood the meaning of X-ray and operation. Late that evening, an air raid alarm was sounded and everyone in the house dashed into the freshly dug shelter under our house. Then we heard the sound of bombs exploding here and there, which was rare. Since we were well tucked away in the underground shelter and heard only muffled rumblings from the bombs, no one took the explosions we heard too seriously. In the morning the next day, however, much commotion was observed around our neighborhood and the news came that the army hospital had been bombed! My father's doctor friend was home and unhurt in the bombing and the army had found another large house for its new hospital. The doctor was already at work at the new location just several blocks away. Aside from the change in location, business was now back in order and they were ready for my surgery. My father's man piggybacked me again to the new hospital, which was a large Korean-style house with a thatched roof and heavy stones making up its foundations. There, I even saw some of the recovering

North Korean soldiers that I had seen at the other hospital. They also recognized me and, as fellow sufferers, said some encouraging words to me as I was carried to what passed as an operating room. A doctor, not my father's mahjong buddy, came in with what looked like a huge syringe and said hello but not much else. Then with army-style efficiency, he poked the needle into my thigh near the infection. I immediately passed out under the effect of the shot. Perhaps an hour or so later, I recovered my senses and looked around. Not much had changed. The hospital seemed just the same as the last time I had remembered it before passing out. Soldiers at various stages of recovery were walking, sitting and lying down everywhere as before. My father's man who had not left the hospital during my operation recognized that I had recovered from the anesthesia. He saw that the infection had been cut open, cleaned out, and bandaged. I was ready to be discharged.

"We'd better get home," he said. Then somewhat in a hurry, as if he had already made the arrangement with the hospital for my discharge, he picked me up piggyback and started walking briskly back home. He had already received instructions for aftercare and had a small bag with bandages and iodine solution in his hand. I would remember the distance as no more than three or four blocks between the hospital and home. When the piggyback duo reached about the halfway point between the hospital and home, an air raid alarm sounded. This 'halfway point' is quite important in this story. The man hesitated, being exactly in the middle of the distance to cover, trying to decide which shelter to run for—back to the hospital or run for the house. As fate would have it, he decided to run for the house, not back to the hospital, and in great haste, he dashed to the house, having me hanging on to his back, the air raid wailing and the fear of getting caught in the bombing tugging at our hearts. Some of our household members were still not in the shelter yet, as it took some time for everyone to get through the rather narrow opening into the shelter. After a hasty family consultation, they decided that I was too fragile, with the fresh cut and all, to be moved into the shelter. Upon this decision, the man carried me to one of the rooms and, leaving me with a bunch of grapes to eat, dashed to the shelter to join the others.

I lay there in the room, eating the grapes, and soon distant bomb explosions could be heard, somewhat rumbling like the sound the day before. I was still too groggy to feel any real fear, and eating the grapes kept me busy. Some small objects, obviously from the bombing, were dropping on the metal roof of our house, as I could hear the clanging. Soon, the air raid was over and our household members emerged from the shelter and inquired about how the recovering patient was doing. Aside from being immobile, I was doing fine, enjoying the grapes and surviving the ordeal in good spirit. But in no time, we heard the news that the hospital that had operated on me only an hour or so ago had just been bombed, and unlike the earlier one, this time the devastation was near total! My household was abuzz with the awful thought of what could have happened to me if my father's man had decided to dash for the hospital's shelter, instead of my house's. (It seems a great deal of historical differences, such as the many great books that I would write, or fail to write, was decided by the small decision as to which way to turn in one's run, forward or backward.) Also whispered and speculated in our household was the possibility that there was a spy in the area who radioed the hospital locations to the bombers. It was just too uncanny and coincidental that two military hospital locations were destroyed by the bombers in two successive days! And I survived both, by leaving the hospitals just in time!

Aside from these events, I recovered quickly from my lymph node affliction and the war went on elsewhere. The North Koreans and the Americans who were now doing the main part of the fighting fought ferociously along the Nakdong River that surrounded Pusan, the North Koreans trying to cross the river and the Americans trying to stop them from crossing. Close to one-third of the Korean population had converged in Pusan, awaiting their fate. The North Koreans, in the meantime, stretched their supply line all the way across the Korean peninsula, tip to tip. This gave General Douglas MacArthur, the commander of the U.N. Forces, the brilliant idea of landing in Inchon, thus cutting the enemy's supply line in half. Along with the broken supply line, the back of the North Korean Army was also broken. Thus, this Inchon landing had the effect of changing the fortunes of the Korean War. The North Koreans, now without adequate supplies, had to abandon their plan to occupy the south and started retreating northward through the mountain ranges in the eastern part of Korea. General MacArthur was so confident of winning the war now that he publicly promised victory before Christmas. Well, of course, history says the general didn't count on the Chinese who sent a million 'volunteers' across the Yalu River, overwhelming the U.N. Forces that had been on the verge of winning the war.

As for me, the little boy recovering from his leg operation, this great shift in the war had no more effect than saying goodbye to the North Koreans withdrawing from Gwangju and then Gwangju welcoming a new conqueror. We could see the City Hall building, not far from our house, hoisting the South Korean, U.S., and U.N. flags and decorating itself with colorful ticker tapes to greet the return of their own South Korean Military. The North Korean Army had occupied Gwangju for slightly over three months. Now with the tides of war turning so swiftly in their disfavor, the North Koreans withdrew without much fight. The city was eerily silent between the departure of former occupants and the not-yet arrived new military—the South Korean Army and the Americans. For me, personally, the exchange of armies in our city had no serious meaning. The North Korean soldiers that I had met, even the wounded ones, were always friendly and nice. I had been getting used to their uniform in my war-related drawings and I was actually sorry that they were leaving. The Communists had committed many atrocities during their occupation, such as executing quite a few prominent local leaders and elders. But as most conquering armies do, they used local proxies, called 'the partisans,' to carry out the atrocities. During the whole occupation, in fact throughout the entire war, I only saw two bodies, which were executed and on display. Whether they were Communists killed by the Liberals, or the other way around, I can't remember.

Of all the soldiers from the north, one particular senior sergeant and my father seemed to have gotten along very well. Although he was merely a sergeant in rank, his position in the military controlled some sensitive functions and information. Whenever he visited our house, our kitchen maid and my concubine mother had heard whispered discussions on matters of receiving the sergeant as if he were a higher-ranking officer and his visits were always a significant event. One time, I overheard the kitchen maid telling my concubine mother that she was on a 'period' and was asking her mistress what to do. My concubine mother whispered back something to her kitchen maid and handed her a set of clean towels. Well, now we were getting ready to receive the new army, the new conqueror, which was coming into the city any minute. The city elders and leaders, who had been hiding from the Communists, were all coming out, waving the South Korean flag to welcome the old conquering army. My father, on the other hand, had been quite visible with his wholesale business during the enemy occupation and mixing rather comfortably with the North Korean Military when it ruled the city. From what everybody could see, his wealth had only grown under the invaders. Soon, the new military came and the city was abuzz with activities, as power changed hands and much activity awaited this change of rulers.

A few days after the city changed its military occupants, we had a surprise visitor. The North Korean sergeant, my father's close friend, now out of his military uniform, came to our house and told my parents that he had decided to defect from the army. Soon, after some serious conversations in whisper, the defector in civilian clothes left. Aside from this surprising development, the first few days with the new army was singularly eventless for me. One army was like the other, other than the uniform, and I rather missed the friendly North Koreans. I went back to reading my books and drawing battle scenes.

A few more days passed and an event took place in my life that dramatically changed everything. My father was arrested by the South Korean Army for the crime of collaborating with the enemy. I still remember with some sense of fear the night when several soldiers accompanied by plainclothes men came to our house and knocked on the door. They announced that they were arresting Father. They handcuffed him and took him with them into the night. For the next ten days or so, we heard no news and the whole household remained anxious and terrified in this uncertainty. After all, it was wartime and a man's life could be snuffed out with the utmost casualness. Adults around me talked only in suppressed voices and I, not knowing enough about what was going on, remained vaguely upset.

It was during this time that I found out what my father's crime was. Three months or so before, the South Korean Military had to withdraw from the city in a great hurry because the Communists were advancing south with incredible speed. The retreating military left behind them a mountainous amount of material goods, mainly rice and fabric, that the South Korean Military had amassed in preparation for the war. The North Koreans, when they occupied the city, found a large cache of such valuables in warehouse after warehouse. The friendly sergeant was in a strategic position to handle these bounties and arranged a business deal with a local businessman, namely my father, who purchased the stuff and resold on wholesale to other businessmen in the city. In doing this, my father made a killing which made him very wealthy. The South Korean Army, upon re-entering the city and investigating what had happened to their cache of valuables, traced the crime to my father.

Father had always been known as a great salesman. He was so good with his sales pitches that he could talk a freezing man out of his tunic. This served him well with the Japanese rulers when Korea was Japan's colony as he got wealthy doing all their government document printing. When the North Koreans occupied the south, he also did great business with the new rulers. He was just a good businessman who dealt with anyone that served his business interest. He would have been just as successful with Americans if he had been given the chance. He simply talked the salesman's talk. This talking skill saved him in this critical ordeal with the South Korean Army. He survived their accusations, tortures, and their noose with his salesman's charm. But at the end, he could not avoid becoming a physically broken man. The soldiers brought him back home one day, but he could hardly walk. It was shocking to see a normally robust, healthy man of early forties barely able to walk. After the release, my father stayed bedridden for some time and recovered some of his health. But soon, it was decided to have him admitted to a hospital run by American missionary doctors who came to the city with the conquering army. It was winter now, and my concubine mother took me to the hospital several times to visit my father. His room was clean and spacious, next to a beautiful garden. I could see snow flurries through the window on the side of the garden, and I felt a deep sense of foreboding sadness. My father was lying in his bed as the lone patient in the room and talked to my concubine mother and later to me. He didn't strike me as a terribly sick person. My concubine mother served him some apple juice that she had made at home by grinding the apples and squeezing the juice from the pulp. When we left the hospital, we passed an office in which an American, obviously one of the doctors, was reading a document on his desk. I had not seen many Americans before and stood there just looking at him. Realizing that a Korean boy was looking at him with intense curiosity, the man got up from his chair, walked toward me, and said with a smile, "Excuse me," and gently closed the door.

With my father's hospitalization, the mood in the house changed. Now, everything was dark and somber, and one by one, our household members left us and went their separate ways. I don't remember exactly how long my father had stayed in the hospital—perhaps through the winter and part of the spring. The conclusion was that he was not going to recover fully, or that he had regained all the health that was possible for him to regain. Some radical decision had to be made. And this radical decision was that the two households, my father's and my Big Mother's, had to be consolidated. Soon, the decision was carried out and I moved into my Big Mother's house. Once these two households were consolidated and became one, my Big Mother now became my *bona fide* 'stepmother,' whom I soon started calling just 'Mother' upon her request. As the matriarch of the expanded household, she was my new mother, in fact, my stepmother. On the surface, she was now finally going to live with her husband in one house. But by this time, he was, although barely over forty, a sick man with little trace of his earlier robust health. In Korean culture, especially among the older generations, it was not uncommon for the husband, who had been living with a concubine for many years, to go back to his original wife when he got old and was sick or dying. Most surprising of all, the original wife calmly accepted this tradition and custom and received her husband for the remaining years. This is what my stepmother did, and my father joined his first wife's household only when he had fewer days ahead than he had in the past.

I am not sure, at the time we moved back into our stepmother's house, if the war was still going on somewhere in the north or had come to an end. Whether the war was still on or had ended, I was just happy that we joined our household with my other family and started going back to school, which had recently reopened. I was now in fifth grade at the elementary school and was thriving as the class valedictorian and getting superb grades on exams. When the two families rejoined into one household, at my stepmother's house, my concubine mother did not join us. She had spent part of her youth with my father as his concubine wife, and now she faded from my life. One day she was my mother and the next day she was gone. There were no goodbyes and no sweet parting hugs. Likewise, the same was with my adopted sister. One day, we were considered brother and sister, and the next she had just vanished from our household when we left Mong-neng-gi, and from my life. Perhaps she was married off, or she became an adult and had to fend for herself. I had no curiosity about her and did not ask her whereabouts.

Although we grew up part of our early lives as brother and sister, I had never developed a personal affection for her. For that matter, she didn't seem to have developed any feelings for me either. My life had become so disjointed, disconnected and unfelt by events and people, that my 'mother' and my 'sister' quietly disappearing from my life had no visible effect on me. With my concubine mother especially, it was in a way quite startling that our parting had been so insignificant emotionally. We had lived as mother and son for half a dozen years, yet, like my adopted sister, my adopted mother and I had developed no deep connections. I only remember one event when I was on the school's baseball team that involved my concubine mother. One day, while playing in the school yard, we broke a window in one of the houses nearby. My concubine mother came to school, apologized to the home owner, paid for the broken window, and treated the whole team to great donuts. This was the only time I remembered her with any fondness. With her gone, I merely joined the new household where my hitherto 'Big Mother' now became my new mother, or technically my 'stepmother.' By that time, with so many mothers of no real memory or consequence, I had become a shy and withdrawn boy with no real emotional attachment to other family members. I was intensely involved in reading and fantasizing, quite detached, even alienated, from the day-to-day interests of the kids my age. As I grew older, I remember being envious of my friends who said, "My mom said this and that," or "My brother did this and that." As far as I remember, I was never able to say such things about my family. In fact, I had family, but emotionally I lived as if I never had one. Emotionally, maybe I didn't have one.

After our rejoining, the new household was bustling again, almost like the print-shop days. In spite of Father's indisposition, some semblance of a happy family seemed to have returned to our house. My father occupied one room, with the Japanese-style hot-tub and bathroom which my stepmother had reinstituted before his arrival, and the rest of the family occupied the other two rooms. One of the two rooms opened to the kitchen where the women in the household prepared our meals. One day, my stepmother told me not call her 'Big Mother' but just 'Mother,' since we were now living as family. So I obeyed her wishes and called her mother from that day on. In my short life of about ten years, I had gone through three mothers—my real mother whom I had, my concubine mother who had come and gone with no emotional connections with me, and my stepmother whose relationship with me was just beginning and was still uncertain. Not surprisingly, I never thought of my real mother. In our new household, Father seemed to recover some of his earlier health, as he sometimes walked to the nearby toy store to buy me the toys of my choice. This sort of simple show of affection from Father, taking me to the store to buy me toys, had never been shown to the other two boys. In this new household, I was still the star, topped in school, and my father's favorite son. My father spent most of his days in his room, rarely going out or meeting his old mahjong buddies.

There was one ritual between my father and me that I always dreaded. It was his intense interest in my schoolwork in which great school performance was always rewarded with pain and punishment. Once a week or so, he would order me to bring all of my class reports and school exams. Knowing what this portended, I would start whimpering as I collected my almost-perfectly-scored reports and exams. My father would flip through all the documents with great interest, once in a while muttering to himself, "Hmmm, interesting. Hmmm, interesting…" and so on. Inevitably, he would find an exam where I missed one point or a report that fell short of perfection. He would call me into his room, and by then I would be trembling with fear. My father would show me these less-than-perfect documents and ask me to explain these defects in my school progress. When the answer was not forthcoming (how does one explain one's failure other than by admitting one's own imperfection?), my father would bring out a square block of wood, which he sometimes used for a napping pillow, and a switch, which he kept in one of his dresser drawers. Without any further command, I would roll up my pants and stand on the square wooden block, trembling and whimpering. Knowing about this father-son ritual, the women in the household would snicker just outside my father's room. Father, carefully inspecting the switch, flexing it and breaking the air with it in a couple of practice swishing, would now be ready to whip me on the legs. But just before he gave me the ritual whipping, my father would deliver me a short lecture on the importance of hard work and discipline. Then the whipping would begin, giving me a sharp sting on my legs with each lash, about on the same level of pain as a sting by three angry hornets. After a few lashes, perhaps four or five, equivalent to attacks from ten to fifteen hornets, Father would stop and would carefully put the switch back in the drawer for later use. I would then leave his room, tears rolling down my face but glad that it was over. This ritual was so predictable and regular that I never felt lingering hurt or bitterness about it. My father had never cared about my half-brothers' school progress and never lectured either of them on the importance of hard work and discipline, accompanied by whippings. This paternal indifference toward my half-brothers was also deeply registered in their hearts, no doubt. But aside from these ritual stings, life went on otherwise uneventfully and I was coming to the end of my fifth grade.

I continued to be an excellent student, almost always at the top of our class of about fifty. Our seats in the classroom were assigned according to our exam results so that the highest scorer would be assigned the desk that was closest to the teacher in the front of the class and the lowest scorer would be the last one in the back, furthest from the teacher's desk. (I am not sure if they still practice such a politically incorrect form of discrimination against slower students.) I always sat next to the teacher because I was always the top scorer. The only time I had a challenger was when a refugee kid from Seoul bested me on an exam and took the desk away from me temporarily. The students who occupied the front row formed a sort of elite group in class with their visible academic superiority. Those who occupied the last row in the back, obviously relegated to academic inferiority, and very likely to a life of simple labor and drudgery, endured the present humility and future obscurity. During the recesses, these academic proletarians congregated in the back of the classroom among themselves, away from the general spotlights occupied by the front row elite. One day, during recess, there was some excitement in the back row of the classroom, which obviously called everyone's attention. Out of curiosity, the elite members, including myself, joined the low-brow group to see what was going on. What had caused such excitement in the back row was that one of the least members was showing everybody that he had mastered the Chinese characters! The Chinese characters! There were thousands of the hieroglyphics so difficult that nobody would dare touch them. This lowest-browed student, who daily endured the humiliation and discrimination of being the slowest student, was showing up everyone with his brilliance. The disbelieving classmates challenged him with difficult words, like 'machine,' 'nation-state,' 'mercy,' and the lowest-brow of our class was writing down, with flourish, the called-out words in Chinese without missing a beat. The least among us was the best! A genius among us! It was too bad that such a genius among us was relegated to the lowest position in our unfair academic hierarchy only because the subject of Chinese characters was not part of our standard curriculum. How unfair life was! When the recess was over, we all drifted to our desks in silence, with a profound sense of shame and thoroughly humbled by the revelation of a hitherto-unrecognized talent among us. What vaguely overshadowed the shocked minds of the young scholars as they slowly moved to their seats was how unfair life was.

I was always active in school sports, and on this snowy December day (just before the start of the winter break which would last through late February), I was playing soccer with my classmates on the school playground after all other kids had left. The snow was so heavy; we could hardly see one another. But we were having too much fun to worry about the snow. Then the school janitor came out of the office and called out my name. I stopped playing and walked over to him.

"Your father is dead," he said. "Your family just called. They want you to stop at your sister's and tell her that…"

I did not hear the last part of his speech clearly. It worried me on the way to my half-sister that I had possibly misheard the janitor. My step-mother's oldest living daughter, who lived near my school, was married to a police chief currently assigned to some rural station. What if I made a mistake with the message, telling my half-sister that father had died when he hadn't? When my sister saw my face, she knew what had happened and broke into a deep heartbreaking wail. I still worried that I might have made a terrible mistake with the message; maybe my father was not dead yet.

When I got home, I could hear the wailing and see the lights blazing all over the house. Indeed, my father had died and I was greatly relieved that I had not misdelivered the death message to my sister; Father *was dead*. In the previous few days, I had no sense that his death was immanent, as he showed few signs that this was going to happen. Relatives and friends congregated for the funeral. My oldest half-brother, who was still in the army in charge of their boxing unit, came home on leave for his father's funeral. I had not seen him for years and he was like a total stranger to me. Now the three sons, all wearing mourners' garments and headgear, stood and wailed whenever friends and relatives came to pay respects. The ritual was repeated whenever a visitor came, donated money, and bowed to the portrait frame of the deceased on the table. The custom called for the sons to wail appropriately, to show their sorrow, along with the mourner who wailed loudly. Sometimes, after so many ritual repeats, I was not inspired to wail or was too tired to wail, and my half-brother would nudge me and fiercely whisper, "Wail!" and I would resume my ritual wailing. Through it all, I felt a vague sense of tragedy and evil things to come, but had no intense feeling of sadness about losing my father. As with my many mothers, I had developed little or no deep affection for my father. My father had never played with me, and his stern Japanese-style gentleman's demeanors had been more awe-inspiring than endearing.

To this date, I have no idea what killed him. It could have been the torture he received while in the military's custody, about which I have no detailed knowledge. He smoked with great gusto, almost three packs a day. But he was only forty-four years old at the time. Could cancer, from his smoking, have overtaken him at that age? The number forty-four subsequently became a milestone for me and I was always worried that I would not live beyond that age. Many of my books were written before I was forty-four, for I was always afraid I might die before writing down all of my important ideas. Once I passed forty-four, I relaxed considerably and my writing slowed.

Father was buried at a public cemetery on the outskirts of Gwangju and, with all the funeral proceedings done and all the relatives gone their ways, my life seemed to return to normal as a sixth-grader. There was the all-important business of national exams to determine which middle school we were destined to attend after our matriculation from the elementary school. The middle school that was everyone's dream was the Teachers' Middle School, which would lead to the Teachers' High School, after which a teaching job was offered. Becoming a teacher, a safe and honorable occupation, was every sixth-grader's dream. It was mine also. I was still the valedictorian and an excellent student, with nearly perfect scores on every exam. Everyone expected my career to be smooth and successful.

But now at home, with Father dead, a very deeply unhappy stepmother was in charge of my life. In a way, it was like the city changing its ruler and occupying army. With the new ruler of the household, the true matriarch of the family in charge, I now had to reckon with a very angry stepmother. Up to this time of her life, she had almost never experienced any moment of happiness as a woman or merriment as a wife. Her husband had always deserted her in preference of a prettier and younger woman, first my mother and then the concubine. Of all the kids he had sired, her husband always took the youngest son, the smartest one, with him to his separate household. No wonder, always solemn and sorrowful, she rarely smiled and almost never laughed heartily. Toward me, she pretended nothing. Although I was a star student at school during the sixth-grade year, she never came to PTA meetings as my mother or guardian. I remember only one time that she showed me any sign of kindness, if not affection. In winter months, the skin on my hands used to bleed with cracks mostly from the exposure to the cold wind. One day, when the bleeding became quite unsightly, she offered to help me soak my bleeding hands in warm water and rubbed the dead skin off my hands with a stone with rough edges. The skin had now been soaked in the water long enough so that the cracked skin could be rubbed off. Doing this task, mother and son (after a fashion) sat side by side for a while like any mother and son. Her tenderness toward me was so extraordinary that, afterward, the very image of my stepmother rubbing the dead skin off my hands, a somewhat painful process, always brought me to sentimental tears. However, my hands continued to bleed and the unhappy woman never again showed such tender mercy toward her stepson. For all practical purposes, I was an orphan whose parents nobody ever saw at school. In such circumstances, I trudged to school, stolid and serious, so rarely exposed to the happiness or frivolity of childhood. Unbeknownst to myself, as a sixth-grader, I was becoming a deeply sad and brooding boy, reading and dreaming to survive his terrible loneliness. At home, with Father gone and with no one to protect me, I was now facing a scorned woman such as hell had never seen before.

During the year following my father's death, my home life was changing radically but under the circumstances, unsurprisingly, from Prince to Pauper. I knew some things had changed after his death. But I didn't have clear ideas what those changes were and how quickly they would materialize, or how dramatically. The very first sign of my tough life ahead came when I broke my left arm while playing with friends in the neighborhood. My arm snapped and in panic I straightened the broken arm myself and, holding it with my good hand, rushed to the hospital next to my house. The doctor, my father's one-time mahjong partner, examined my arm. He concluded that it seemed set straight by my own emergency handling. As there was not much a doctor could do, he sent me to the neighborhood bonesetter to handle the rest. (At the time in Korea, broken bones were handled by bonesetters). The local bonesetter looked at it and said that it was set so straight that he didn't have to reset it and told me to come back in a week or so to make sure everything was all right. To my surprise, my stepmother refused to pay the bonesetter's fee, a relatively small amount, in spite of my pleading. And out of shame, I never returned to him for his re-examination of my broken arm. The bonesetter lived only half a block from our house and rather than walking past his office, I would go around another block to avoid the embarrassment of running into him. Luckily, my arm healed without further issues, but I never paid the man for the first visit and it remained my permanent scar of dishonor as long as I lived in the neighborhood.

Other refusals followed. One of her most crucial refusals had to do with my career. She refused to pay the tuition to the Teachers' Middle School, whose entrance exam I had passed with flying colors. Only one other student from the elementary school passed the exam with me. It was such a celebrated promotion to a career-assured middle school and her refusal truly devastated me. In fact, she forced me to talk to the principal at the Teachers' Middle School and ask for his mercy by exempting me from the entry tuition, since my father had died and left me destitute. In compliance, I trudged to the Teachers' Middle School every day but either did not have the courage or was too ashamed to beg the principal. It was a hot summer, and I would simply sit at the school playground and would trudge home when it was dark, hungry, and tired from the struggle to collect enough courage for the begging. Most galling, my half-brother was the star basketball center, for his towering height, at the Teachers' Middle School. (At the time in Korea, basketball games in middle and high schools were played outdoors.) I could see his team practicing not too far from where I was sitting. Yet, my athletic star half-brother never acknowledged his little brother sitting there in such misery. He practiced with his teammates and left the practice without the slightest glance in my direction. To my stepmother's ire, I never managed to ask the principal for his special exemption. Of course, my stepmother, as my mother or guardian, neither volunteered to go with me nor helped me with my cause in any way. Perhaps she wanted my education to stop at the sixth grade (which it eventually did). The deadline for paying the entry tuition passed and my precious career opportunity was all for naught.

She even refused to pay the yearbook cost so that I could not be with my schoolmates for the yearbook picture. When my half-brother joined the Boy Scouts, she refused to pay for my uniform so that I couldn't join. She simply said no. Horror of horrors, one day she had a shoe shiner's box built for me and demanded that I become a shoe shiner. When I absolutely refused to take up the new profession, she demanded that I sell newspapers. She proceeded to buy ten copies of the newspapers as a trial case for my new career as a newspaper salesman. Selling the newspapers involved walking up and down the alleyways shouting, "Newspaper! Newspaper!" But I could not sell a single copy on the first and only day of my newspaper-selling career. She was furious when I brought all ten copies of the newspaper home, scolding me severely that I had not shouted loud enough. After this failure, she then demanded that I collect firewood in the mountains. I obeyed by going to the mountain, along with many other poor kids, but came home without a stick of wood. One failure after another, I was now enduring the wrath of a very unhappy stepmother with an agenda for her stepson who was failing at so many different ways of earning a living.

Misery loved me in another way at this time. I was bitten by a dog in the butt. Coming home from school one day, I decided to take a shortcut by going through a courthouse which had a huge yard in the front with hardly any human traffic. I didn't know that there was a vicious dog there which was very unfriendly to human traffic. As I was unconsciously walking through the yard, minding my own business, the unfriendly dog dashed out from nowhere, fiercely growling at me. Instinctively, I started to run, hoping to outrun him to the street where people could help me. The dog was obviously faster than me. He caught up with me long before I reached the street and bit me in the butt, which started bleeding through the pants. Hearing my scream, an adult ran out of the building, shouting at the dog, at which point the attacking dog left me. The adult took me to the water pump nearby and helped me wash the wound. The hurt from the wound was much less painful than the fear that my stepmother would be furious with me for the incident, although it was not my fault. Fortunately, the tear in the pants was much smaller than I had feared. There were just two or three holes where the dog's teeth penetrated the pants. As I limped home, I never told my stepmother about this incident and nursed the bite on my own. Eventually, the bite healed without anybody noticing it. Providence helped me once again, because the dog-bite could have killed me with rabies. Apparently, the canine attacker was not a stray dog and was free of rabies. Even now, it makes me shudder just thinking about how I could have died from the bite.

My half-brother, now taking the cue from his mother, joined her in her meanness toward me. Perhaps all the bitterness of an unloved son toward the favored one was now unleashed. He was tall and played basketball at his middle school and was constantly in need of extra food, which, unfortunately for me, he supplied from *my* rice bowl. As he and I were served at a separate table from the rest of the household, with nobody watching us, he would scoop out almost half of my rice and put it in his bowl. He gave such a fierce look of threat that I couldn't say a peep about this regular food expropriation. Surely, my stepmother must have recognized this pitiless and regularly-occurring action by her son. Such obvious food commandeering at every meal could not go unnoticed. But she pretended not to notice. Since rice was the main staple in our diet in those days, I was losing close to half of my daily nutrition to my half-brother under the pain of terror if I said a word about it. This regular loss of food was existentially painful to endure and I was always hungry for food.

My half-brother terrorized me in another way. After my father died, my step-mother decided to enlarge the house to accommodate her daughter's family to join her household. She did this by taking out all the Japanese-style space-eaters built into the house, such as the indoor plumbing and hot-tub. This renovation meant that the household now had an outhouse in place of its indoor plumbing, which was built on the left side of the house. This outhouse became a new source of suffering for me because it revealed what a coward my half-brother really was. Unlike what he appeared to be on the outside, the great athlete and tough guy was, after all, scared to death of going to the outhouse by himself at night. (I should have known considering the way he reacted to the senile lady during our evacuation stay at the farmhouse.) Whenever he got the number-two urge, which seemed to come always in the middle of the night, he would wake me up and make me sit on guard outside the outhouse door. All that I remember is how freezing it always was when I had to squat and wait out his nightly bowel movement, shivering and shaking in the cold. Sometimes, after he had done his number-two and got hungry, he would make me climb up the fence and pick a persimmon or two from the tree in our neighbor's yard that leaned over to our side of the fence. Cold and the fear of falling off the fence were an evil combination that I suffered under the terror of my cowardly half-brother.

Every day became a terrible torture to endure from so many sources. One of the things that I found especially torturous was a daily verbal attack from my stepmother. Every day, when I came home from school, my stepmother would call me in to her room and would start her daily narrative. Generally, it started with all the evil faults of my father: how they married when he was only twelve and she only sixteen; how he ran away, only returning home to make a baby; and how, in all their lives, he always found another woman, leaving his wife alone with the kids in misery and desolation. Then the subject would turn to my real mother who had vanished from my memory and had become a non-existing person. Since to exist is to be in memory, she didn't exist for me because she was not in my memory. The stepmother's daily attack on my mother had no effect on me any more than being attacked by a shadow boxer. One of my mother's most grievous faults, which this unhappy first wife repeated over and over, was that my mother would get up in the morning and fix the breakfast for her husband without even washing her hands first. My mother's lack of hygienic consciousness was something that had stuck so deep in my stepmother's heart that she made the same comment over and over, without even consciously thinking about it or making any attempt to vary the description.

"Imagine that," this unhappy first wife would wail to me, "fixing breakfast without washing her hands!"

Unlike her two sons, who had strongly resembled her husband and were tall and strong, I had the misfortune of inheriting my mother's more delicate island look which was more tropical Asian than most Koreans. Daily, my face reminded the stepmother of the misery and unhappiness my mother had caused her (although the last six years or so were due to the concubine wife, since she had taken my mother's place). Her unsophisticated farm-woman look was somewhat inferior to the more sophisticated but illegitimate wives. There was no suffering greater than for a woman to be scorned by younger and more attractive women. The man who had caused this was dead now, as was my step-mother's own happiness. Daily, I was the living reminder of who had caused her lifelong suffering, namely my mother. But fortunately, I was protected from this verbal assault by not remembering anything about my mother. Whenever my stepmother said, "Your mother did this," or "Your mother did that," it hardly occurred to me that she was referring to my own mother. I had never once thought of her as a real person. The very concept of 'mother' was non-existent as reality and as memory. I had three mothers in my young life, but I might as well have grown up with none.

As far as my memory was concerned, I was born without a mother. I was only three or four when she left me after World War II. Then, the devastation of the Korean War that killed three million people made death and disappearance a routine way of life in Korea. Someone disappearing or never coming back was so common that such was hardly anything to talk about. I simply counted my mother as one of those who had vanished in the war. Fortunately for my mental health, her non-existence, in reality or in memory, never caused me any emotional trouble in my young life. I was simply surviving in the world of my book heroes and fantasized realities.

However, the daily misery I received from my stepmother did inspire me to hate my father. My hate toward Father was not moral, as I was too young to form moral judgment at the time about the deeper meanings of scorned women, but financial and immediate. He left me financially destitute and with no protection from my stepmother's attacks that he should have, or must have, anticipated to come after his death. He could not have died without anticipating the inevitable hardship that would come to his favorite son. I had dreams virtually every night whereby I found out that he had left a huge fortune just to take care of me. Waking up to the miserable reality of the morning, from the happy nightly dream, was perhaps the most painful part of my daily routine during my entire sixth grade.

With my father's death, and being left helpless and powerless to the whim of a very angry stepmother, my life as a young orphan was being sucked into the vortex of an unpredictable existential reality. Truly, hell knows no fury like a woman scorned, and my stepmother, scorned and furious, was now an angel straight from hell, seeking vengeance. It was now becoming an urgent bread-and-butter survival issue as my stepmother's attacks were becoming truly terrible, first with hurtful words and then in mean actions. Providence endowed me with the gift, or curse, of stubbornness with which I was struggling to hold up under the daily assault of my stepmother. She had not given up the hope, and effort, of turning this gifted scholar into a successful shoe shiner.

Under my stepmother's daily assault, my days were becoming more and more hopeless and demoralizing. I was mostly hungry from not having enough food due to my half-brother's regular exploitation. My clothes were hand-me-downs from my half-brother, which were mostly ill-fitting and worn out from the former wearer's active athletic life by the time I inherited them. But I never got to inherit his Boy-Scout uniform because the activity had not been there long enough for his uniform to become my turn. It would have been thrilling to wear even a worn-out Boy-Scout uniform. My shoes were alarmingly tattered in spite of my constant repairs with needle and thread, and ink to smudge over the repair.

Walking to school and trudging back home in the afternoon, I cut a rather pathetic figure. I was demoralized with hunger and shame. After I trudged home, I would be predictably summoned into my stepmother's room. There I would face her day's haranguing about my mother who had given her so much misery. I was the recipient of her daily living wrath from hell. Tired and hungry, I would often fall asleep during her long angry lamentations, which further fired up and energized the angry stepmother. For a boy who had grown up with books and imagination, somewhat shy, unassuming, and well protected by his wealthy father, there was no hell like my step-mother's fiery hell and there was no relief for me. As they say, I could neither run nor hide. My obstinacy, stubbornness, and strength from my own fantasy world of books and imagination were wearing thin. My own survival, both physical and mental, hung in the balance. I remember coming home from school one day and finding no one at home. It was deserted and silent. I was overcome by some primeval grief of loneliness that had been held up inside for a long time. I sat down in the yard and sobbed uncontrollably for the next hour or longer until somebody came home. Otherwise, no one ever saw me weep so openly, before or since.

It was about this time that I started going to church, in particular a Presbyterian church not too far from home (coincidentally, right next to my father's old print-shop building). My sudden religious inspiration had nothing to do with spiritual conversion but with urgent existential issues. The U.S. government, feeling guilty for forcing South Korea into an indecisive truce with Communist China—South Korea's president Syngman Rhee was raring to continue the war with North Korea and China—decided to pacify the Koreans with food and money aid. In this effort, the U.S. poured into Korea generous military K-rations left over from the war and other food aid. Helping with war orphans was particularly popular in America. One of the items for food aid, which was sent to Korea in great quantity, was dried milk. This dried milk, which could be dissolved in water as milk or just simply eaten as a snack, was distributed to poor people through the protestant religious network. The Presbyterian Church next to our old print-shop was one of those designated for the dry milk giveaway. It was this milk largesse that had inspired me to attend its Sunday school and learn about Samson and Jesus.

The church bell rang at the crack of dawn and I got up from my warm bed and, shivering, walked to the church for my reward from heaven. Chunks of dry milk, my Earthly reward from heaven, were given out at the end of each Sunday school. I later dissolved the dried milk into boiled water, with cheap saccharine to sweeten it, and made hot chocolate, except there was often no chocolate. You could also eat it by scraping and shaving the hard chunks with your teeth to enjoy the milk nutrition. This gift from America created at least one Christian boy who learned about the heroic tales of the Jews and Christians. Eventually, I graduated from Sunday school with a certificate to prove my religious attendance.

There was actually one more non-spiritual purpose, for which I attended the Sunday school religiously. Out of shame, more than anything else, I never told this to anyone, not even to my closest friend. It was, aside from the dried milk, my primary goal for church attendance: getting better footwear, namely shoes in better condition. My shoes were always worn to shred, and it was my great dream to get good shoes. I remember, during a heavy rain, I found a good-condition shoe drifting in the rainwater, which I eagerly grabbed. But in spite of my frantic search, high and low, the other shoe was never found. The result was that I had to live with the full sorrow of having just one good shoe. (One good shoe is the most useless, regretted item in the world, unless you are a one-legged person.) This shoe problem could be remedied as a reward for attending Sunday school where some boys came with decent shoes. The strategy was that after the school was over, you would rush out, spot a pair, and take off with them. Of course, you could never go back to the same Sunday school again with someone else's shoes. But so starved for better shoes, I was willing to stop coming to church once I had obtained a pair. I would have much preferred to find a good pair of shoes than a good trip to heaven. For one reason or another, however, I was always one of the last to leave the sanctuary and what was always left there was my own tattered pair of shoes that nobody would have wanted. Not for want of trying, I still never succeeded in expropriating better shoes. As a result, I learned more about Samson and Jesus by continuing to attend church in search of those shoes. The dried milk remained the main consolation for my spiritual quest. (At the time, I had no idea about what my father had left my stepmother in the form of wealth. But my stepmother had not seemed too inconvenienced with her finances, considering the way my half-brother enjoyed his life, joining the Boy Scouts and all.) Slowly and miserably, my sixth grade was over, and since I had paid no entry tuition for the Teachers' Middle School, my formal education ended on the day my sixth grade ended in March, and I was eleven.

In the meantime, one good news we heard was that a philanthropist in the city started a tent-school where kids who could not attend a regular middle school were given an unofficial education. I managed to attend these classes where they taught English and seventh-grade math, which attracted a few poor kids as my new classmates. Often, the enterprising classmates at the tent school, most of them equally hungry, decided to pilfer some of the barley grains that were ripe in the nearby fields. Roasted over open flames to burn off the husk, the barley tasted good and staved off some of our nagging hunger. Some of them were quite professional in the arts and sciences of pilfering food growing nearby and agreed to have me tag along as their tender-foot novice in the skills of survival. I learned some other rudimentary survival skills, verging on delinquent or even criminal, which helped me later when the challenges became greater. At home, my life had now changed dramatically, from an academic star to a shoe-shiner candidate and then to a tent-school student. Things didn't look too bright for me in my prospective future.

Then, one day, a pivotal event occurred. We had a surprise visit from my concubine mother. She had heard of my father's death, a year after the event, and came to pay respects. The two former wives of the deceased, the source of so much bitterness and unhappiness for one, now as two widows of the man who had caused all this, seemed to unite as two victims. After the ritual wailing at our makeshift memorial altar, the two women withdrew to the inner room and talked for some time. Here was a woman who had been my *bona fide* 'mother' for half a dozen most tender years, and yet there was not a hint of gladness in my heart to see her again. There never was a hug or kiss from her during our years as mother and son. She lived with my father and left him when he was ill, all according to some contract she had signed with my father when she had agreed to be his concubine wife. Little me, a five-year-old boy, extraordinarily clever and largely adorable, was just a collateral part of the agreement. It was as if the contract did not include any personal affection with the collateral clause.

From what I learned later, after she left my father when the two households had been consolidated, she found another man of considerable age as his new concubine wife. Her new contract husband, a widower, had a son who was doing well as the director of an orphanage. The war had produced so many orphans that taking care of them naturally became a good business, especially with ample financial help from the guilt-laden U.S. The 'orphan business' was now an emerging lucrative enterprise in the war-torn nation. When my half-brother and I heard that my former concubine mother's new 'son' was an orphanage operator, we were quite impressed. Of course, I had no idea how that simple fact would affect my own little life so profoundly.

After the first visit, as if the ice had been broken, my former concubine mother visited the widow more frequently now. Obviously, the death of my father, the final end of a prodigal son, had closed chapters on both women and they could now be on the same side. More and more conspiratorial, each time they withdrew into the inner sanctum, they talked for a long time. Having developed no emotional undercurrents with my former concubine mother, I paid no special attention to her rather frequent visits and long whispered talks. Still, some sense of mystery hung around these visits and the low-voiced conversations between the two widows. Whatever it was that they talked about so secretly, for some reason it didn't seem to bode well for my own welfare. This ill feeling was a product of the simple intuition that I had garnered from my life with them that neither of these two widows had any abiding affection for me, nor did they have my interest at heart. Neither of them had ever loved me, I was sure of it, and now their present conversations didn't change my sense about them. One day, the wall of mystery finally broke. My stepmother called me into her room soon after my former concubine mother left.

"You know she has a son who owns an orphanage," my stepmother said rather solicitously. He 'owned,' not 'ran' or 'managed,' an orphanage. I said I had heard of it. "They get a lot of money from America and all the kids there eat well and attend regular schools."

Here was her final solution. She wanted me to go live at the orphanage! My former concubine mother's connection would fix the paperwork and I would go there as a war orphan. Technically, this was true. My father died during the war and I was an orphan, but only technically. My stepmother drove home the advantages that I would enjoy there at the orphanage, like good food, good clothes, and regular school to attend. But given my upbringing, I was strongly prejudiced against the very enterprise of orphanages. I would rather die than live in an orphanage, and even thinking of myself as an orphan was something I could not accept. The very idea was repugnant. The orphanages were for kids that were not only without parents, but also without any hope of salvation. They were former thieves and delinquents, riff-raffs of society nobody wanted. Unlike them, I had hope (not sure what kind of hope) and I was going to be salvaged (not sure by whom or what). I kept refusing her offer to go to the orphanage, though she promised to give me some spending money if I agreed. The last item of offer was really difficult for me to refuse.

This pressure to agree to go live at an orphanage increased, more so each time the former concubine mother visited the current widow and had one of their conversations. Factually, I might be an orphan, to be sure. But I had grown up quite sheltered and well-nurtured until recently. Much of my young life had been lived as the favored son of a very rich man, and the very idea of living as an orphan among the formerly street urchins was totally out of the question. Yet, the resolve of a proud eleven-year-old boy to stand fast to his idealism and dreams in the face of the lure of spending money was under a severe test every day. The force against him was administered by a very determined, scorned woman whose hellfire would not rest until its target was scorched and melted down. My misery was compounded from every source, increasing the pressure to escape. I even started wondering exactly how much she was going to pay me if I agreed. The vision of tasting some cakes and sweet potatoes that I could buy with the spending money was just too much to resist every day. Napoleon once said that soldiers marched on their belly. He could have also said that hungry boys march to orphanages on their belly as well.

"Yes, Mother!" I finally hollered one day, "I will go to the orphanage! Yes, I will go to the orphanage!"

I had finally succumbed to something that many millions, perhaps billions of brave men in history had succumbed to—money and food. The imagined pleasure of money and food, the two classic lures of men and boys, was just too much. I sold my pride and honor for money and food. Instantly, my stepmother became very nice and fed me full meals, and miraculously, peace was restored in the house. My life became tolerable as the two widows made the arrangement. Like a man on death-row enjoying his last meal and civility from the executioners, I was suddenly very loved and everybody was sweet to me. It was in the middle of winter when it was snowy and freezing everywhere, compounded by some sort of a gasoline shortage in the country that stopped most vehicular transportations. Could the trip to the orphanage be postponed until spring? The women saw no transportation issue. "No problem," the two women assured me. The director of the orphanage, technically my stepbrother (After all, he was the new son of my former concubine mother.), would make sure to arrange the necessary transportation and pick me up personally, and very soon.

I gathered a bit of information about the orphanage, as I was getting ready to enter it, located about a hundred miles away in a small city to the west of Gwangju and about thirty miles to the north of Mong-neng-gi, my beloved fishing village. The city was called 'Yonguang,' meaning 'glory,' and years later, the town was advertising itself to tourists as 'the City of Glory.' Of course, there was nothing glorious in my association with the city. I learned that the fifty or so orphans who were there called the director of the orphanage 'Father.' My one good school friend, who had heard of my impending departure, teased me that the director was not my father; he was my 'brother.' My new father-brother had arranged a truck and was coming for me in a few days. Apparently, because of my association with *his* new concubine mother, who used to be *my* concubine mother, I was treated as a special case. A major change in my life was about to begin; I was going to an orphanage. While waiting for the trip, I still felt terribly unsettled, in spite of the sudden peace and good food. Everything seemed temporary, and something not to my liking was going to unfold.

It was a snowy, cold day in February that the director of the orphanage came to pick me up in a truck with a driver. He was a relatively young man, perhaps in his late thirties, with signs of well-fed and well-dressed prosperity, brisk, and businesslike. I was slightly disappointed that he didn't treat me as a special acquisition case, as, after all, I was technically his brother. Besides, I was no ordinary orphan, a sheltered, previously favored son of a rich family. Apparently, the orphanage business was pretty good for him. To validate my impression, he stopped at a watch shop and bought himself a new watch, paying for his new watch with cash which he counted out from a wad he carried in his inside coat pocket. I was very impressed by this demonstration. (Memory is a highly selective thing. I remember the orphanage director rather vividly to this day, but I remember nothing about the truck driver. He was a complete persona non grata in my storage of memories. Maybe the truck was driverless.)

The drive was slow and torturous because of the snowfall, which made the going difficult. During the hours we were on the road, the orphanage owner never talked to me, as if I didn't exist. The roads were virtually empty of traffic because of the paucity of vehicles in operation. By the time we arrived in the City of Glory, it was getting dark. The snow was deep as we plowed through it to reach the orphanage just outside the city. The somewhat-unfriendly reception of me by the director and the dark and desolate landscape outside the lonely truck plowing through the snow made me terribly unhappy about the prospect ahead. Somehow, I felt it was not going to be something sunny and happy that I would face at that orphanage. Everything seemed foreboding and mean.

As we approached the compound, I could see a throng of bustling humanity forming shadows and figures with lights from bare bulbs hanging here and there in the yard. Recognizing the director's homecoming, the orphans and adults shouted their welcome as our truck moved in and stopped just inside the gate. As I got out of the truck, I could smell something pungent and quite revolting as if they had slaughtered a wild animal and were preparing the meat. Under the lights and in the darkness, the orphans, who were lined up there for dinner, looked at me with cursory curiosity. Somebody told me that the orphans (I cannot remember if they were co-ed or not.) had captured a deer in the nearby mountain that day and were having a venison supper that evening. So the deer meat was what had offended me with the wild smell. By then, I had been exposed to some unusual foods, with the help of my pilfering classmates at the tent school, but had never smelled, much less eaten, wild animal meat. They gave me a plate and motioned me to line up for my turn to receive the food. This new experience churned my stomach and I could not eat even a bite of this celebrated meat supper. I had sold my pride and honor for this food! Everybody seemed too excited about the deer meat to pay attention to this new kid. After supper, everyone drifted to their rooms and I was assigned a room with half a dozen boys. I had brought a small bag with some changes of clothes and several books, one of which was a novel about two doomed lovers that I was currently reading. Still, nobody talked to me or asked me questions. After trying to read a page or so further about the doomed lovers, the warm room and the day's ordeal overcame me and I fell into a deep sleep.

I woke up to the first day as an official member of the orphanage. The winter break from school was still on until March, so most boys had to go to the nearby mountain to collect firewood as their day's task. An older boy told me, as we were climbing the mountain that was not too far from the orphanage, that I didn't have to collect any wood, since it was my first day and I was from the city. (Of course, they didn't know about my non-productive one-day excursion into collecting firewood under my stepmother's direction.) I felt miserable with my new life at the orphanage that was just beginning, which was quite alien to me. The boys looked awfully uneducated and ill-mannered, looking truly like the orphans of the war who had survived the worst of everything. By comparison, in spite of my recent misfortunes with my stepmother, I had been delicately raised and treated while my father was alive to protect me, not exactly suited to this rough-and-tumble life at an orphanage. I had already read *Oliver Twist*, and other books about orphans and orphanages, but what I saw here was just too rough to endure. As the boys were collecting firewood and checking to see if they had trapped another deer, I was dreaming that my one good friend had organized a rescue party to take me away from this infernal place. I was lonely and sad, and their regular meals were so unpalatable, and my heart so broken, that I could not eat for the next few days or sleep for the next few nights.

I finished reading the book about the doomed lovers, who eventually committed suicide at the end by taking poison. Their revolution had failed and the lovers lay dead side by side in their boat as it drifted out to sea. This story further intensified my misery, and I decided I had to escape. This was not my life that I had foreseen while growing up with books and dreams, and with the prospect of great things to accomplish in my future. I was paying the price for failing to resist my stepmother's pressure and her seduction with money. I had to run away.

Three days passed since I had joined the orphanage and nothing improved. My loneliness and sadness were painful and their food, or my taste for it, had not improved. On the fourth day, I gathered my things in the bag and waited for the best time to break out. Ever since I had arrived at the orphanage, nobody paid particular attention to my escape. I had not seen the director since the day he had dislodged me there. Nor were there any officers of the institution who paid me even the slightest attention. If I had walked out in broad daylight, nobody would have stopped me or recognized me. Still, I hardly slept that night. There was a bit of guilt I felt toward my father-brother who had taken the trouble of bringing me to his orphanage as a favor to his own new concubine mother. And I was paying him back by sneaking out without saying goodbye. But the situation called for stealth and resolve.

I woke up on the fourth day, just as the dawn was cracking, and, grabbing my bag, I quietly got up and left the room. The boys were still in deep sleep, some of them snoring. I walked out the door into knee-deep snow and freezing February air. It was impossible to find the road we had taken to get to the orphanage. I guessed the general direction of the town and took a straight line through the field toward the City of Glory. To my short height, the snow was so deep that I had a tough time just trudging through it. The unevenness of the field caused me several falls as I was trying to find the hard surface to walk on. Still, I made good progress (Perhaps the distance to the town was not as great as I remember it now.) and I could see the downtown buildings ahead. I even found a small roadside vendor inside a tent so early in the morning, getting ready to open up their odds and ends to the customers. They had some rice cakes and I bought several pieces with the money my stepmother had given me, and I devoured them with relish.

Fortunately, the gasoline shortage had apparently been lifted as the vehicle traffic was now busy again. As I neared the vicinity of the town, I saw a truck onto which two men were loading up sacks of rice, one man on the truck receiving them and another man on the ground throwing the sacks to the man on the truck. I waited there watching the men until they were about done with their loading.

"Sir," I said, approaching the man on the ground, "where are you going?"

81

The man looked casually at me and said, "Going to Gwangju."

I was lucky. They were going to Gwangju. "Can I ride with you? My family is in Gwangju."

The man wasted no words and simply motioned me to climb up onto the truck. With their help, I climbed up and lodged myself in a crack among the rice sacks. Thankfully, the sacks were made of soft cloth, not of the straws called 'gamani' that Korean farmers commonly used. In fact, the crack I decided to settle on was quite comfortable and in no time my lack of sleep caught up with me and I fell into a deep slumber even before the truck started moving.

"Hey, boy!" the truck driver hollered, startling me from my deep sleep. "We're in Gwangju now."

The truck had reached its destination. I didn't realize that they had covered the truck with a thick dark tarp, in effect, keeping me warm and comfortable during the ride. I crawled out of my spot in the truck and jumped off on to the ground. The truck had stopped on the road by the river and I recognized where I was. (If I had walked a mile or so south on that road, I would have reached my old home with the air raid shelter.) I thanked the men and they drove away. In those days, there were so many young boys on the loose that goodhearted people, like these truckers, helped them in any way they could without asking questions.

Now, I was back home, but I could not go home. The wrath that my escape from the orphanage would invoke in the stepmother was just too much to contemplate. I couldn't bear the likely consequences of her wrath. Fortunately, my good school friend, whose parents operated a small inn, was nearby. Not having the courage to go back home and face my angry stepmother, I spent the night there in one of the empty rooms at the inn. I was happy to be out of the horrid orphanage, but I could not go back home. It was an uneasy, fitful night of sleep. I had no idea that my little life was coming to the end of one chapter and beginning another that very night.

III. The Street Urchin

After an uneasy night, and spending all day with my good friend discussing the best way to assuage my stepmother's expected wrath, we decided that I had to go home and face the music. I tried everything to slow down my walk home, stopping at every bookstore on the way just to delay the inevitable. I thought up every possibility—maybe another war, an earthquake—that would slow me down on my way home. Still trembling in uncertainty and fear and hesitation, I trudged the few blocks between my good friend's inn and what had been my home until recently. It was late afternoon and getting slightly dark when I finally reached the house. It seemed that over the few blocks, I had never come home so quickly before. I wished the house was a hundred miles away so that I would not have to get there so soon.

There was a relatively large yard between the house and the gate which remained mostly open because there was no bell on the gate. Visitors and vendors would just come through the gate and then knock on the foyer door to announce themselves. During warm months, my stepmother used half of the front yard to grow vegetables and the other half for a flower garden where she planted many different flowers, especially big red and white dahlias that bloomed so abundantly and beautifully in season. There was a pathway that ran from the gate to the house, and my stepmother planted noon flowers along both sides of the pathway, which bloomed all summer. She was a great gardener and the yard was almost always filled with one kind or another of vegetables and flowers. But such a wonderful lover of nature was so full of venom and hate toward her stepson, or what her stepson symbolized to her. Just now, covered with snow, the yard had neither flowers nor vegetables.

With great foreboding, I entered through the gate and, like a condemned man approaching the gallows, slowly walked toward the house. All was quiet and I didn't see any sign of human activity in the house. From the gate, I had seen the smoke coming out of the chimney, which indicated something was cooking in the kitchen. So, I quietly walked around the right side of the house toward the kitchen. (On the left side was the infernal outhouse that kept me shivering and trembling under my half-brother's order.) In the kitchen, busily cooking was my stepmother, who was stoking the fire under the cast-iron rice cooker with a metal poker. I stood at the entrance to the kitchen, somewhat prepared to spring to action. My stepmother, sensing the shadow behind her, turned around and faced me. Blood drained from her face, which instantly turned into a pure rage. Here, standing at the door to the kitchen was the devil himself, returning to torment her. She had thought him safely gone, out of her life forever. Like her worst nightmare, the devil was back!

She shrieked something unrecognizably animalistic and, grabbing her poker frantically but firmly, lunged at me with all her might. Obviously, she intended to strike me with the poker, no doubt with all the strength she could muster. If my stepmother was a pure animal in her rage in attack, so was I in my defense. Fortunately, I had been anticipating this, and I was not lacking my own animal instinct for survival. Fight or flight, as they say. I chose flight. In spite of all her rage and fury, she was an older woman and I was a young boy with speed and agility on his side. I escaped her first lunge and then turned around and ran toward the gate and then out. My stepmother gave a good chase to the gate and I could hear her fierce groan that was not intelligible, not even human. After I was safely out of her sight, she locked the gate and presumably returned to her kitchen.

For the next ten years, this was the last I saw of my stepmother. When we met again, it was a circumstance that even a seasoned dramatist could not have imagined. Nor did I ever meet my concubine mother again. Apparently, my disappearance from the orphanage had not created any questions or inquiries. I had become a *persona non grata*.

Several times, after my stepmother's poker attempt on my life, I tried to rejoin the family. But each time I tried to enter through the gate, I found it firmly locked. It no longer stayed open. Nobody in the house ever answered my pounding, sometimes crying, sometimes crying out, to open the gate. I could hear sounds and see light in the house, mostly happy and warm, but the gate remained closed for me. My stepmother's second daughter (The oldest daughter had died in childbirth years previously.), whose police-chief husband was always assigned to rural posts, had moved into the renovated house and her three young children had added a considerable activity and gaiety to their home life. But I could not be part of that happy family. Often, I stood there at the gate, exhausted from pounding it and crying, thinking that something was wrong. Some mistake had been made regarding me, who was actually a high prince, and this would be a great story to tell someday. Already at this age, I was fighting my real misery with the device of imaginary fairytales, stoic detachments, and heroic triumphs.

At such times, when I was pounding the gate and crying, one of the neighbors unable to bear the suffering of the young boy would come out and take me into his home for the night. But my neighbors were never judgmental toward my stepmother. Perhaps knowing the misery and unhappiness that my father had caused this widow who was their longtime neighbor, they decided that I was merely paying the price for the sins that my father had perpetrated on the widow. If someone had taken me to the police to complain about the mistreatment of a minor, the policeman would have agreed with the unhappy widow. Yes, the boy deserves to be cast out as the retribution for his father's sins. Shouldn't the sons pay for the sins of their fathers? In the aftermath of chaos and disarray from the war, the law had no business meddling in such petty family matters.

Among the good neighbors who took me into their house was a man who worked as a chef at a restaurant, who one day asked me if I wanted to work there. By then, I had no other choice. I had already quit going to the tent school and, without a home, and having run away from an institution, now I had to fend for myself. During the next year, I followed the chef to several restaurants and worked as a waiter, kitchen help, and handy man (or boy).

Normally, I slept where I worked, as they provided the room and board for the workers in lieu of wages. This way, I at least secured room and board and escaped from the intense winter cold. My stepmother and I lived in the same city, but we never saw each other, as if the other didn't exist. I did not stay in the orphanage, but as far my stepmother was concerned, I had never returned from the exile. I just vanished from her life and that was all that could be wished for. Part of the price of my father's sins was being paid off in his favored son's retribution.

(There was retribution in another way. This part of my life, being kicked out of my home with nowhere to turn, became the source of my lifelong recurring nightmares. Even after I had become a secure professor at an American university, I was plagued with the nightmares because I couldn't control my unconscious life. The contents of the nightmares were mostly the same. I would be out in the cold, somewhere on the street, hopeless and desolate, wondering where I was going to find shelter. In the back of my mind would be the thought, even in the dream, that I was now a professor in America and why would I still be on the street, homeless and desperate? This nightmare stopped only when I passed forty-four, finally surpassing the age at which my father died.)

Sometimes during these days of my early life in full employment, my elementary school classmates, generally goaded by my inn-owning friend, would visit me where I worked. They were in regular middle schools and living under strict control of their parents. Thus, my homeless lifestyle, working for my own room and board, away from parental control, was something of a grand independence.

When I had time off from work, we would go out and have a wild reunion. They also took me to a night school in the city where different subjects were taught free of charge for the poor kids who couldn't afford regular schooling, similar to the tent school except on a smaller scale. I took full advantage of these opportunities and attended as many of these classes as I could. My favorite subject was English and, with my eagerness to learn, and being a quick study, I was already becoming the volunteer teachers' favorite student.

It was about this time that a popular western movie, *Shane*, came to Korea and it became to me, in a lasting way, the symbol of all that was wonderful about America. The story itself was simple. A retired gunfighter seeking peace comes to this Wyoming valley. There, he settles to become a farm hand and help a homesteader and his family. But in spite of his desire for peace, he is drawn into the conflict between the ranchers and the farmers. In the end, Shane fights his last battle against evil and, after a tearful scene with the farmer's boy who begs him to stay, rides into the frontier myth.

The Hollywood movies, especially those produced during their Golden Age, became my lifelong passion. Those movies were the source of a great escape for a homeless boy of my sensitivity and imagination and were still made with celluloid film. Because of its bulk, only one set had come to Korea, to be shown in its capital city, Seoul, first, and then shown in lesser cities in subsequent runs. Each time, because the celluloid strip had to be run through the lenses, the film added more scratches and sometimes blackouts when the film broke. When this happened, the screen would go blank as the film broke. Then the projector-man would reconnect the broken film and resume the projection, always losing a few frames in the process. The audience would groan but patiently wait until the projection resumed. One of my friends who had gone to Seoul had seen *Shane* and told us all about the grandeur and majesty of the west and the appealing hero who was played by actor Alan Ladd. As the film had not come to Gwangju yet, I envied my friend who lived in Seoul, working at a beef-jerky factory, for he could see all the movies before us. I wanted to go to Seoul and work at that beef-jerky factory, which to me sounded like a dream life. My friend promised to help me find a job at the factory if I came to Seoul. The desire to go to Seoul was thus planted and I was thinking about it subsequent to our talk. Eventually, *Shane* came to Gwangju and I saw at least the upper half of the movie, since the theater was standing-room only and I was just too short to see anything but the blue sky in the movie. I was thrilled when I finally saw the whole movie and became a lifelong devotee of Alan Ladd. To me, *Shane* and Alan Ladd were indistinguishable, and the actor and the role were so seamlessly blended that it was hard to tell where one ended and the other began. In the ensuing years, I saw *Shane* close to a hundred times, generally at the fifth or sixth-run theaters where the film was all scratched up and constantly interrupted with film breakage. It didn't matter. I loved the film because of its essential representation of the days of simple justice and goodness. To me, such was the essence of the America that I imagined and yearned to see. Shane became my idol and hero—brave, chaste, and gentle—and I wanted to be like him. Whenever my morale was sagging, through the vagaries of my life, the image of this perfect hero helped me regain my strength. In my later professional elitism, I pooh-poohed the influence of Hollywood, but deep down, I was hopelessly affected by one of its masterpieces and master-heroes. This idealized version of myself was radically removed from reality because I was still a homeless boy, surviving each day precariously. Even in my fantasies and dreams, America was like a mirage in the desert, all the more cruel and pitiless because my real life was so miserable.

(As an aside, years later, I wrote about Shane *as the quintessential American hero in a chapter, titled* 'The Hero in Art,' *in one of my books called* Art, Beauty, and Pornography. *Actually, being my bestselling book whose sale was bolstered mainly by its title, I sent a copy to George Stevens Jr., son of George Stevens who directed the movie. Stevens Jr., who was then the head of the American Film Institute, appreciated the gift and sent me, in gratitude, a biographical video about his famous father. My connection to* Shane *did not end here. Still more years later, my son Jonathan entered the Stark Film School at the University of Southern California as a graduate student [over my objections, as I wanted him to stay at MIT and study science, not decadent Hollywood]. To my surprise and delight, his masters' thesis was directed by Professor David Ladd, the son of Alan Ladd who played Shane. If the reader can imagine the poor kid in Korea, soon after the Korean War, in tattered clothes and worn shoes, sitting in dark theaters to watch* Shane *and admiring Alan Ladd, the eventual connections with its director and actor are quite*

astounding, even uncanny. Indeed, what are the chances that fifty years later, the son of this poor orphaned kid in post-war Korea and the son of Alan Ladd, the Hollywood star who played the hero in the movie, would be connected by pure coincidence as professor and student? But we are still in Korea in this tale and it is still just after the war.)

Although I was not starving and was earning a living in the restaurant profession, my vision was still something grander than that. Most of my friends were in school and in spite of their admiration of my independence, it was a heroic life without a future and in abundant present misery. Especially since I had talked to the beef-jerky friend who promised to help me find a job in Seoul, I was strongly affected by the desire to go there. Another push that turned me toward the capital city, perhaps more direct and immediate, was on my back, propelling me forward. The restaurant owner was a man of some influence in the Liberal Party, the main political party in Korea under Syngman Rhee and backed by the U.S. As such, his restaurant enjoyed a considerable unofficial patronage of the ruling political party's members. Many city and province politicians patronized the restaurant on credit and one of my jobs was to visit them and collect their debt once a month. The owner, who earlier had a son in my sixth-grade class, knew about my life before my stepmother and treated me with kindness and trust.

But my life at the restaurant was still hopeless. One of my routines was to take the trash out to the river and illegally dump it early in the morning before anybody could see me. I used the restaurant's bicycle to carry the trash box to the illegal trash dump at the river. I had to walk the bicycle to the river because it was old and the chain kept slipping. The dump site at the river was only about a block or so from my old house where I had lived with my father during the war years. Every morning, I passed by the house, pushing the bicycle with the trash box, thinking about the days I used to live there as the son of a very rich man, and being bitterly aware of my present misery.

One day, the local newspaper announced that the new movie house wanted, as its publicity stunt, an open contest for its company logo, with considerable award money going to the winner. For some reason, I thought I could win the contest with my design entry. With the win, and its award money, perhaps I could seek a new fortune in Seoul. The only catch in this contest was that each entry had to be accompanied by an 'entry fee,' which in today's amount would be close to twenty dollars. Of course, I had no such money. After some serious thinking about it, I decided to use part of the money that I collected from the Liberal Party members who paid me at the end of each month. Since I was going to win the contest with my superbly creative artwork, I would just simply pay back the expropriated money with the winnings. In confidence and assurance, I entered the contest with my superbly original logo design, accompanied by the entry fee, and awaited the happy announcement that I won. Well, to my surprise, I did not win the contest. In today's more sophisticated world, one might have smelled a scam, but I was innocent and believed in honor and justice. But this turn of event was a devastating disappointment for me who had counted on the winning money. Aside from my artistic failure that was bad in itself, I had the impending financial disaster that demanded that I had to have the expropriated money by the end of the month. Now, I had a more immediate reason to escape to Seoul and find another financial source for the train ticket.

At the time, the capital city of Korea, like most large cities in the third world, was something of a contradiction. On one hand, it was a city of opportunity where ambitious people tested their fortunes in the hustle and bustle of city life. On the other, it was a city of misery and evil where innocence was destroyed and corruption underlined the façade of the surface shine and light. Today, it takes slightly more than three hours' drive from Gwangju to Seoul on a first-rate freeway. But in those days, it took all night for the coal-burning 'night train' to reach Seoul, chugging along and stopping at virtually every town on the way. Still, it was the cheapest way to get to Seoul, which seemed like another world so far, far away. It was the cheapest way for sure, but I didn't have that ticket money. So, I schemed to get some money. I decided to rent a bicycle, ride to the train station, and sell it for the ticket. I figured that by the time they discovered I had not returned the bicycle on time, I would be on the night train to Seoul. This was an air-tight scheme that could not fail, or so this young genius thought. Obviously, I had not learned about the dangers of self-confidence and assurance from the logo-contest experience.

There was another motive for me to target the bike shop as my victim. Revenge was involved. It goes back to my sixth-grade days when we were busy getting ready to take national placement exams to get into the pivotal middle-school choice, which would take only the top students. I was approached by a teacher who asked me if I would switch my exam with another student by writing his name on my paper. This scheming teacher was a third-grade homeroom teacher whose office kept the school's only mimeograph machine; that was one of its earliest prototypes. Since I was the class valedictorian and the best brain, I was assigned the duty of mimeographing the day's homework for our class. In this function, my job consisted of writing down the homework on the wax paper with a sharp pen which scratched the wax off the paper. When this was completed, I would attach the wax paper to the metal frame with a heated iron. The melted wax around the edges of the frame would stick to it when cooled. Then I would place the stack of white paper under the frame and roll the wax paper with an ink-soaked roller, printing out each sheet underneath until enough copies would be done. I did this virtually every day and the mimeograph-keeping teacher knew exactly when I would come down to his classroom to do the job.

On that particular day, the scheming third-grade homeroom teacher said he wanted to talk to me after my printing job was done. Somehow, I knew it was something not honest. He laid out the plan. The student and I would switch our names on our respective exams, mine on his and his on mine. I knew the student because he was in my class where I was the class valedictorian and the top student. He was not very bright, most of the time sitting in the back of the class, and could not enter a school of his choice on his own. The third-grade teacher, who had the scheming classmate's sister in his class, said that the student's family was rich and they would pay me, a poor fatherless kid, good money for my trouble. He asked, "Why would you need to score so high on this exam? You could take other exams and

do well later and attend any school you want at a later date."
Feebly, I told him that I would think about it. Such schemes
were not uncommon and rumors about them were heard
around school. Bright but poor kids like me were especially
valued for such easy schemes of switching names. When I
returned to my classroom, pale with fear and anxiety, my
own homeroom teacher sensed that something evil had
happened. He took me aside and asked plaintively.

"Do you want me to go to prison?" he asked without
wasting words. "If you do anything bad, that's what will
happen to me. You must tell me what you discussed with
Mr. So-and-so."

I dearly respected my teacher because of his fantastic
'Jisan-bop' (doing math calculations with one's fingers). He
would hide his fingers behind his back and when the
numbers were called out, he would beat us all who were
doing the same calculations on the speedier abacus. This
show always entertained and impressed us. Now, today I
was part of a criminal scheme to dishonor my beloved
teacher. I broke down and started crying and confessed the
whole scheme concocted with the corrupt third-grade
teacher. My homeroom teacher listened and had me swear
that I would do no such thing. For good measure, my
homeroom teacher dictated to me a note to the dishonest
teacher to say that I would not participate in his scheme and
the partner, the rich kid who wanted my brain, would not
write my name on his exam. The note was delivered to the
scheming teacher, and no more was heard from him. The
partner, whom I saw in our classroom virtually every day,
acted as if nothing happened, but avoided eye contact. The

incident was soon forgotten and we were busy with our national placement exams for our individual futures.

That rich kid's family in the failed plot owned the bicycle-rental business and it was one of their bicycles that I was going to steal. A year or so after the foiled scheming, my fortune had changed, for worse. Now I was in a desperate position to procure the train ticket, scheming to concoct a crime for which I had previously accused the kid. But hypocrisy was a luxury and I could not worry about it at this desperate hour. I would like to state that I wanted revenge and justice for all the trouble he had caused me when we were in sixth grade. (Perhaps I should have gone along with the scheme and received some money, considering what my situation turned out to be.) But in actuality, such noble thoughts had not been my motive. I just needed the ticket money to go to Seoul, and after the logo-contest debacle, I deemed stealing and selling the bicycle was the easiest way. I had already been homeless for over a year, and drifting through different restaurants for survival had hardened me somewhat with the finer points of morality. My delicate side of books and dreams, where I wanted to be like the great hero, Shane, was being severely put to a test by my reality.

The day on which I decided to enact my plans finally came. First, I wrote a letter to the restaurant owner, confessing my crime of using some of the money I had collected. Since my crime would be discovered in a few days, I wrote that I would not be able to bear the shame of my misdeed. So, with my abject penance and sorrow, I would be leaving his employ and someday I would make amends for my utterly shameless act. I ended with the declaration that I had not done anything else to disappoint his trust in me, etcetera, etcetera. (Years later, my good friend whose parents owned the inn, who was also a friend of the restaurant owner's son, relayed the story to me that when the owner's family read my letter of apology, the son muttered to himself, 'I am sure he (me) will accomplish great things someday.' When I heard the anecdote, it put a much bigger burden on me to truly 'accomplish great things' in my life.)

But their confidence in me to accomplish great things was still decades into the future for me to prove. For now, shameless and desperate, I had to steal a bicycle to escape to Seoul. I easily rented a bicycle, somewhat new and one that could fetch a good price, and started immediately taking off toward a train station in another town, about five miles from the city, where the night train would stop. I had not counted on how tough it was to ride the bicycle over such a long distance. It was late night, in fact close to the time of the night train to stop at the station, when I finally reached the destination. I was looking sweaty and dirty, with guilt written all over my face when I took the bicycle to a bike shop near the station and offered to sell it. The owner looked at me up and down with some care and didn't seem to be convinced that I was the legal owner of this good-looking bicycle.

"Are you sure you are the rightful owner of this bicycle?" he asked me with suppressed suspicion.

I said firmly, "Yes, sir, I am the legal owner of this bicycle, and I am ready to go to Seoul on the night train." He hemmed and hawed for a while, looking at the bicycle this way and that, and he came to a conclusion.

"If you are the legal owner," he said, "would you mind if I call the police station and confirm it?"

"Sure, go ahead," I said casually, but actually my heart dropped to my toes.

Not just that the police station would confirm that the bicycle in question was not mine, the police chief was my brother-in-law, the husband of my older half-sister, my stepmother's second daughter! She was the same half-sister to whom I was quite afraid of having misdelivered the message that Father had died when he might still be alive. My stepmother had the house renovated after my father died, essentially to accommodate her daughter's family when her son-in-law (my brother-in-law) was assigned to this small town as police chief and he preferred to get room at the station. The result of all these family decisions was that the bike-shop owner was about to call the police station whose chief was my brother-in-law, in essence to report a bicycle thief. I met the police-chief brother-in-law only a time or two in my whole life because I always lived elsewhere with my father. The thought of being handcuffed at my brother-in-law's police station was more than I could bear. I was a bicycle thief but had some sense of personal conscience and family honor. The shame of facing my brother-in-law as a criminal would have been so intense that I would have been happier to just kill myself.

The bike-shop owner went into his office to make the call, or so it seemed, and in that split-second window of opportunity, I made my escape and took off, of course without the bicycle and without the money. I ran as hard as I could toward the train station which had no fences on its backside. I had been quite surprised that the owner of this tiny bike shop was so honest. His honesty apparently paid off, as I left the stolen bicycle as a gift to him for his honesty. Reaching the station, I went around to the backside and walked to the platform where the night train was going to stop. There was no sign that either the bike-shop owner or my police-chief brother-in-law was after me. In fact, that late at night, the station and its vicinity were pretty quiet. But to be safe, I stayed out of sight until the train arrived.

The night train that traversed from the southern tip of Korea to Seoul, the whole length of the peninsula, was the microcosm of post-war Korea itself. It was the train that carried people, who were hopeful and hopeless, prayerful and desperate, to the capital city in search of a better fortune. Some of them would find more hospitable luck than before, but many would become victims of schemes and frauds. Many boys would become hustlers and thieves. Many girls would become prostitutes and low-brow workers. The night train, slow and crowded, normally had more people standing than sitting. Because it was burning coal for fuel, the black smoke from the coal belched into the train cars and made everyone's face black whenever it went through a tunnel. People took their handkerchiefs and towels out to cover their faces, but the smoke had nowhere to go but to be blown back into the train. Some passengers would attempt to sleep, but those standing would just have to stand until they reached their destination. The train would eventually reach Seoul early morning, and the passengers, miserable and tired, would be disgorged and dispersed, each one to their own destiny.

The night train eventually arrived and I emerged from my hiding place to board it. In the meantime, more passengers had arrived at the station and waited for the train on the platform. I boarded the train along with them. There was no ticket-check at this point. That would come later. I found myself a space in the corner of a car and the train chugged out of the station. Train venders with snacks and drinks passed the aisle with their narrow carts, repeating their offerings in a sing-song voice. The local sellers hustled their cakes and rice rolls, waving and shouting outside the window whenever the train stopped at a station. Soon, a commotion started in our car, which meant the ticket-check I had been dreading was taking place. I dashed toward the toilet and hid myself in a small space nearby that seemed to be out of the way. Obviously, the ticket-check conductor also knew about the little hiding space where many others had also tried to hide when they had no tickets. He came into my space and, finding me there hiding awkwardly, asked for my ticket. I didn't have the ticket because I had failed to sell the purloined bicycle. The conductor, a swarthy, short man slightly taller than myself looked at me intensely as if to decide what to do. Here, he was my judge, my jury, and my executioner. Then, he decided to execute. He slapped me a swift and hard one on my right cheek with his open palm, which made me stagger, because I had not expected it, and I fell to the wall. He looked at me with strong official disdain, his eyes then softening to pity, and then abruptly walked out. With the sting of the slap still felt on my cheek, I assumed that I had paid for the ticket. Indeed, there was no more ticket-check that night and I arrived in Seoul without further payment in punishment. My night train had disgorged me in this capital city, early morning in shiver and hunger, and I had no idea what fortune or misfortune was awaiting.

As the passengers from the night train were moving through the gate, I was greeted by a sharp-looking young man who asked me if I was cold and hungry. There were other greeters who were picking their targets, some young women and some boys like me, asking if they were cold and hungry. I must have said yes, although I don't exactly remember what I said. As a result of our conversation, I ended up following him out of the terminal. Many others, boys and girls, had also found their guides and were doing likewise. As expected, Seoul was a bustling metropolis, crowded, busy, and dusty with traffic even at such an early hour. Actually, aside from this impression of crowd and traffic, I remember very little of what I saw as I followed the sharp-looking young man who was good enough to welcome me to the city. Nobody had ever warned me of the pitfalls in the capital city and I had no fear of the man's intentions. In spite of the mistreatment I had received from my stepmother, and he experience as a restaurant worker, I was still trusting of strangers and unsuspecting of life's vagaries. We must have walked a few blocks from the train station when we reached a house much larger than an ordinary family home. He invited me into the house and served me some hot food in one of the rooms that was warm and cozy. There were some vaguely uncertain activities of people, mostly young boys and some adults, in the house. There was an air of conspiracy and jubilation, neither of which was openly discussed or demonstrated. Much of their excitement seemed suppressed. The sharp-looking young man told me I could lie down in the room and take a nap

102

since I had not slept all night. I did as I was instructed. I fell asleep instantly after I finished the food.

It was somewhat later in the morning that I woke up from my sleep. There was more of the suppressed rustling that I had observed earlier around the house, some young boys about my age and some a few years older, chatting and laughing as if they had just witnessed something exciting. Other than a quick look at me, just like the reception at the orphanage in the City of Glory, they paid me little or no attention. One boy in particular was demonstrating something, and other boys around him were laughing. The boy made a loop with somebody's long hair and, hooking something up with it from the person's upper pocket, grabbed it as it flew out of the pocket. The demonstration indicated that the boy had taken someone's pen from the pocket using a hairy thread to hook the object and yank it out. This was done in such a swift motion and with an almost-invisible loop that obviously the victim had no time to react to this form of pick-pocketing. They were pickpockets and they were boasting about how they victimized 'Americans' in particular. There was a huge U.S. military base near the train station and the Americans stationed there were easy marks. Yes, I had been brought to a den of pickpockets for a career as a street thief! I had read about such characters and, although I was poor, hungry, and jobless, my goals in life were much higher and possibly nobler, maybe even like Shane's. I realized what they were up to, and I was taking no part in it. I just walked out of the house of thieves.

My most urgent business was trying to locate the friend who promised to help me find my ideal job at the beef-jerky factory. Somehow, I could not find him or his beef-jerky factory. The address that I had for him was vague and even the local boarding-house realtors did not remember if there was a beef-jerky factory anywhere in their neighborhood. Maybe it was an illegally operating underground factory where the owner didn't want the law to know what they were doing. Maybe they were using illegal horse meat to make beef-jerky products; the speculation was wild. But there was no beef-jerky factory, legal or illegal, anywhere to be found, and giving up on finding the ideal employment, I was on my own.

The next few months, I did my best to survive in the streets. (I think it was few months, but I am not sure. It could be much longer or it could be much shorter.) One of my most tried-and-true techniques was book-stealing. I would visit one of the many book stores in Seoul, that was almost always crowded with readers and visitors. Highly inflamed with the passion for education, Korea was crazy about books and acquiring knowledge as a way to advance in society. Parents would sacrifice virtually anything if education for their children demanded it. Years later, passion for education was widely recognized as one of the number-one reasons for Korea's amazing advancement to the ranks of affluent nations. The educational zeal was also responsible for my own survival, as books were not only extremely popular, but they were also easy to steal and turn into petty cash. Pretending that I was a buyer, I would skillfully swipe a book, hide it inside my jacket, and walk out. The crowd, and my own small size, always helped. There were many bookstores which gladly bought such stolen copies from the book thieves like me. One book bought me enough food for a day or two, and I resorted to this easy way of living without conscience. A couple of times I was caught, and both times I would drop the book on the street and run. Happy that they retrieved the book, they never pursued the thief. Sometimes, I would hit upon an old lady who kept a little mom-and-pop street-corner vendor with comic books. As the old lady was distracted by other customers, I would quickly snatch a candy bar or two and put it in my pants' pocket. Sometimes, the owner would catch me and furiously inspect my pockets. But by then, it would be at the bottom of my pants' leg because the pocket had a slit and the stolen article would fall to the space between my pants and their liners.

I slept wherever I could and ate whenever I could. I was always on the street, walking sometimes and riding the streetcars sometimes from one corner of Seoul to the other, which was the Han River where the street car reached its terminal and turned around to go in the other direction. Unlike now, the Han then had a huge sand beach that occupied about two-thirds of the space between the two riverbanks. Crowds gathered in the summer in lieu of going to the more expensive ocean beaches. Having no place in particular to visit, I often ended up at the Han beach to spend the day, just watching the families and the crowd. I was a classic post-war street urchin by then, with tattered, dirty clothes and a dark face from the days in the sun.

One day on the beach, I was sitting on the sand, cutting a very pathetic figure, eyes wandering but looking at nothing in particular. A young man, a college type, approached me and engaged in a conversation with me. Obviously, he knew I was one of those homeless drifters, always hungry and miserable. He pulled out his lunchbox from his book bag, offered it to me, and sweetly told me to eat, and that I needed it. It was one of those typical Korean-style lunches, what the Japanese call a *'bento,'* which had rice in the main compartment on one side and several side dishes, mostly kimchi, fish, or meat, in a smaller compartment to go with the rice. When the young man gently pushed the open lunchbox under my face, I started crying. The tears were so uncontrollable that they poured into the lunch directly below my face. Soon, I was eating my own tears, mixed with rice and side dishes. The young man watched me eat and started talking about how important it was to be inspired to work hard and not to give up hope. I hardly heard what he said, as I was busy weeping and eating. The man never asked for my name and never gave his, and although I went back to the Han many times thereafter, we never met again. Maybe he was an angel who was sent there to feed me and give me encouraging words.

It was about this time, just once in my entire life, that I contemplated suicide, purely as a protest. I decided that the world was cruel and cold and nobody paid any attention to me. *Would they pay me attention if I tried to kill myself?* I wondered. At the time in Korea, a sleeping pill called 'Seconal' was a popular medicine to induce sleep. It was also known to kill you if you took too many. Virtually every day, the newspapers carried stories of people who committed suicide taking a few of those Seconal pills. It was so popular that even a kid could go to a drugstore and ask for a Seconal for his mom or dad. To keep it somewhat under control, each drugstore was allowed to sell only one pill to each customer. I was not sure how many I needed to kill myself. Maybe ten? By the time I visited about seven drugstores, I got tired (For some odd reason, two of them refused to sell it to me.) and decided that was enough for me. I took the five or so Seconals (The rumor was that some drugstores sold sugar pills to those obviously suicidal-looking.) and positioned myself on a back-alley street nearby a house and swallowed those pills. Some of them were genuine sleeping pills, as I dropped fast asleep.

Someone was shaking me up, hollering, "Hey, boy, wake up!" I soon struggled up to a sitting position. Obviously, members of the nearby household came out and were trying to wake this fast-asleep boy. I doubted they knew if I had taken pills to kill myself. Several faces were surrounding me with anxious and curious expressions, watching for my reaction.

"What day is it?" I asked, as that was all I could muster. They told me it was Tuesday. I had taken the death pills on Monday and was now waking up on Tuesday! I had slept exactly one night on those sleeping pills! I was dead for just one night! Suddenly, a feeling of embarrassment came over me. I bolted up and, kicking away the clean blanket that covered me, obviously supplied by the family, staggered out onto the street and went away. This was the only time I thought about killing myself, and I never tried it again. Did I really try to kill myself? No, I just wanted to call attention to my loneliness and the struggle I was waging alone in this world. That's all. I just had too much to accomplish. It was not my destiny to kill myself.

Eventually, I found a suitable job at a factory, but one that was not making beef-jerky products. It was a family-owned factory that produced fluorescent light fixtures, which had become popular recently because of its power-conserving advantage. The factory had been built adjacent to a family home so that the building was used by the factory on one side and by the family on the other. There were about a dozen boys, mostly older than me, under the direction of a very kindly foreman who had learned his workmanship in Japan during WWII as a slave laborer. The technical supervision was carried out by the owner of the factory who worked along with the employees, teaching and directing various parts of the manufacturing process. One of the boys who watched me being introduced said loudly, "He is an Indo-jing!" meaning a 'blackie.' It took two weeks or so of staying indoors for me to return to my normal pale skin. And the boys stopped calling me a blackie. I was immediately put to work, operating a press that cut the specially treated E-shaped metal pieces around which the copper coil would be wound to specification to transform the electric currency to fluorescence. Cutting the E-shaped metal pieces was one of the easiest jobs which I was assigned. The press machine had two parts. The lower part had a hollowed-out E, the female part, while the upper part had the E itself, the male part, which would slide into the female E in perfect precision. As I pressed the machine with my right foot, since I was right-footed, the male E slid down into the hollowed-out female E as a perfectly fitting pair of E, the male and female parts. As the press operator, all I had to do was put a piece of metal over the female E and press the foot pedal. Then, as the male E slid into the sharp-edged female E, the metal piece in the shape of an E would drop into the waiting basket on the floor. I repeated this all day. The work was easy but tediously repetitive. There were many parts to the whole process before the finished product was packed into the cardboard box to be shipped to the market. But mine was the simplest and easiest for a young novice worker to get started.

During the breaks, the boys would gather, standing against the front wall outside that had been warmed up by the sun and enjoying the warmth. In front of the factory, on the other side of the entrance driveway, was a beautiful mansion where reputedly Korea's most famous actress, named Jo-myryung, lived. (In Korea at the time, as in Japan, as there were no strict zoning laws, the rich people lived near poor people and even small factories). The gate always stayed locked and we never saw the famous actress in person. One of the older boys, with a somewhat unappealing face, declared that he wanted to be a movie actor when he grew up. The grimy-faced boys with factory dirt on their clothes all expressed the dreams of what they wanted to be when they grew up. The former WWII slave-labor mechanic sometimes joined us and once said he wanted to have his own shop someday. He was very wonderful with the boys and entertained us with his stories of survival as a slave-laborer that he had endured during WWII. Although some of his stories were quite grim and harsh, he seemed to have retained little or no mean residues from his suffering. Some boys said they would want to work for him when he had his own shop. I had no idea what I was going to become when I grew up. My dream of going to America to become a famous professor-writer was about as farfetched as the boy with an ugly face wanting to be a movie star. My most urgent goal was working hard to master the technique of winding the copper coil around the metal pieces so that I could escape the drudgery of the metal pressing work. Often, the two daughters of the owner, the older one about my age and younger one still in elementary school, came out and joined the boys. Together we all lined up against the wall in the warm sunshine and speculated on our futures. I was not sure what I was destined to become, but I knew I wasn't going to be a factory worker making fluorescent lights for the rest of my life.

Before I mastered my coiling technique, however, I became the victim of a small accident. After so many *E* pieces were produced at my machine, I would bring another large sheet metal to get the whole process started again. While I was routinely carrying a large oiled metal sheet to my presser machine, which I did many times a day, this time it slipped through my hand. As I instinctively tried to catch the heavy metal sheet, it cut through my right hand, leaving a deep and long gash between the thumb and the flesh of the palm. (The scar is still visible to this day.) I was disabled for a while, which didn't please the owner. Unable to master the coiling job, I was back to the press machine as soon as my injury healed. But another injury followed on the press machine. Whenever you pressed the machine to cut another *E* piece, you had to be careful to keep your fingers away from the pair of *E* cutters, male and female. The pair would mercilessly slice up whatever else that got in the way of the pair. Since you repeated the same moves all the time, your moves became automatic so that your fingers were out of harm's way a split-second before your foot pressed the machine. Accidents occurred, of course, when these automatic routines were violated for some reason. It happened to me as I pressed the cutter without being in full coordination with the hand. In short, my foot and my hand failed to coordinate their split-second moves. The result was that the machine cleanly sliced the tip of my left middle finger, and I lost about half of the fingernail of my middle finger. (It still hurts sometimes.) The doctor said I had microscopically escaped cutting my bone. But aside from this lucky break, he couldn't do anything about the finger, since the sliced-off portion was gone and there was nothing that he could stitch up for me. He sent me home with some bandages and boric acid to clean it up every day, dressing the cut with a new bandage. For the next few weeks, I dressed the wound in excruciating pain, as the bandage had stuck during the night to the flat surface of my cut-off fingertip. It was an agonizing process to wet the bandage and pry it slowly and painfully off the cut. (Medically speaking, the question of why I did not keep the bandage away from the cut surface never occurred to me. Maybe bad advice from the doctor?) Often, fresh bleeding would follow the dressing routine and I would curse my fate and destiny for such a miserable life. And I was barely thirteen!

My hand injuries, coming one after the other, caused the owner much inconvenience. It naturally caused me much inconvenience also. One of the most immediate difficulties as a result of my hand injuries was my inability to deploy my fingers for lice-hunting. We boys, about five of us, who stayed at the factory for our room and board, all roomed together and one of our leisure activities consisted of engaging in lice-hunting. The lice (its singular form is louse.) were the most common and pesky insects that took advantage of the people like us who lacked regular baths and changes of clothes. They prospered on human blood and dead skin by residing in the seams of unclean undergarments. We, of course, singularly lacked trips to public bathhouses, which affluent Koreans enjoyed at least once every three days. Three days of wearing the same underwear, especially among active laborers, might be the minimum hygienic requirement to keep the lice away from the human body. (Today, most Koreans shower once a day.) We often spent weeks without a trip to the public bathhouse. The result was that the lice prospered on our blood and dead skin and multiplied their population at the underwear seams. Most outward symptoms of lice infestation was the frequency of scratching to counteract the itching that the lice caused in our crotches. Lice-hunting, aside from the practical benefit of fighting the pesky insect, also served some sort of psychological function as outlets for our poverty and powerlessness. Before we went to sleep most nights, we took our underwear off and began our nightly lice-hunting. Under our bright fluorescent lights, we would hunt the lice and pop them with our thumbnails. The most efficient method of destroying the lice was putting one louse at a time between our thumbnails and pop it until it broke the insect up into pieces with a loud snap. The experience taught us how to pop it without letting it slip, for sometimes, thumbnails became quite slippery with blood from the executed lice. The more the louse was full with our blood to the point of being fat and round, the greater was the pop it generated, and the more final the execution we enjoyed. The psychological effect was quite deep and satisfying when we killed those lice that had lived off our blood and had gotten fat and round. Sometimes, we had a contest of whose pop was the loudest, or whose thumbnails were bloodiest from the slaughter. We gleefully chased after these helpless lice infesting our bodies and mercilessly destroyed them as their sole judge, jury, and executioner. Aside from the inconveniences of my injured hands, I participated in this rampage of slaughter with relish.

Then, after a few months of uneven accomplishments at the fluorescent-light factory, word came from somebody that a wealthy family in Yongsan, a district of Seoul near the Han River, was looking for a houseboy. When this job opening was confirmed, I immediately announced my departure from the injury-prone manufacturer of fluorescent lights. The two daughters of the factory had become quite fond of me by then and were sorry to see me go. But the owner was happy that I was no longer there, much of the time injured and unable to work as fully as my room and board would demand. We said goodbyes and I collected my meager belongings and rode the streetcar to Yongsan to meet my new master's family where I would serve as their houseboy. Three lovely girls, all under about five, greeted me with their shy chatter along with their mother, a very beautiful stately lady who looked at me with some interest as if she had questions about me.

"I know you," the mistress of the house finally said, after all of our introductory preliminaries were out of the way. "You used to come to my father's hospital with your father to play mahjong."

I then realized that the pretty young woman that I had seen sometimes watching us at the hospital had now become my employer. I was not totally unhappy at this discovery. It meant that the mistress of the house now knew that this street urchin who had come to her house as a servant had some elitist pedigree which one time equaled her own. By the quirk of misfortune, namely my father's untimely death, however, I had become the houseboy of her household. In spite of my low-brow life, or perhaps because of it, I had become exceedingly sensitive about pride and dignity. So, it was good for me to discover that my employer's father and my father were mahjong buddies one time. In the long run of harsh economic reality, this past equality in social class meant little or nothing. I was still her servant now. But at the moment of our introduction, this little bit of salvation meant a lot to my pride and dignity.

Their house was a large two-story wooden structure with many rooms that had been built by the Japanese. Unlike the traditional Korean style of heated floors, many of the rooms had *tadami* flooring, the sections made of rice stalk. I was assigned a small room on the ground floor near the side entrance, with a barred window to the street that was mostly busy with soldiers on leave. (Yongsan was the designated train station for the military personnel and my new employer's house was only two blocks away from the train station.) During the day, the neighborhood was like any other, busy with humanity and surrounded by family houses and their children, rather inconspicuously normal. But at night, its character changed completely—lights suddenly blazing and streets suddenly crowded with working women and soldiers on leave. The working women emerged from everywhere and nowhere, actively soliciting their soldier-customers coming and going. A typically respectable neighborhood, in which my master's family house was nestled, became an actively brazen marketplace of prostitutional traffic. Strangely, this mixture of prostitution and a stately household with young girls, all in one neighborhood, seemed perfectly normal. It was as if there were a cultural agreement between the neighbors during the day and the prostitutional business at night, and neither would cross into the other. Neighbors refrained from being judgmental, showing great respect for the working women in their struggle for survival. The seedy night people were careful not to intrude on the respectable neighborhood. No snide gestures or comments were ever made toward the working women who carried on with their business in utter professionalism and discretion. It was a nation just after the devastating war where everyone was trying to survive and there was no room for snide elitism or moralistic judgment.

The mistress of the house explained my duty as primarily taking care of the girls. On the side, I would keep the yard in the back of the house clean and sweep the two streets on the front and side once a day. In addition, she explained that the master, a contractor dealing with electric insulation, might need me to travel with him, carrying odds and ends, such as transformers and insulators, for his business. Otherwise, I was an all-around houseboy who remained handy for any household task. The first two or three nights were somewhat strange because two of the household maids, for some reason, had to spend the night in my small room. The three of us, one boy (me) who was just entering puberty and two girls in their upper teen years, filled up the whole space in the room. The smell and sound of the two young (older than me) girls kept me stirred up all night. Thankfully, they soon found their own room and left me alone.

My job required taking the little girls to the park across the busy boulevard for an afternoon outing. The small park had the usual swings and slides, and sand lots, for little kids. On one side of the park was the busy boulevard and the city, and on the other, a barbed-wire fence that was the border between Yongsan and the U.S. Military's residential block. The American Army, so full of mystery and exotic culture, stretched from one side of the city near Seoul train station to Yongsan where the barbed-wire fence ended its stretch. Sometimes, as my girls played on the swings and slides and sand lots, several American girls of similar ages would appear shyly near the fence. Recognizing the visitors on the other side of the barbed wire, the Korean girls would walk up to them on our side of the fence and stare at the American girls. Both groups of girls, not being able to speak to each other, would just stare at each other, not in an unfriendly way, and often just smile. Soon, the American girls would be called away and this meeting across the fence would end. The fence was hardly scary or overdone, like the fences at Auschwitz, God forbid. But in a symbolic way, the fence divided, just in the space of few yards, two completely opposite worlds of reality. Indeed, on one side was the world's greatest power, the rich Americans, and on the other were the poor remnants of the war that had destroyed virtually everything. These occasional encounters with the American children intensified my yearnings and dreams for a paradise called America.

My experience as a houseboy had its unintended benefits. Several college students, close relatives of the family, occupied one of the rooms in the house and they turned out to be the treasure trove of my precious

116

knowledge. I read virtually all the books they had in their collection, which was beyond what my hotel-owning good friend in Gwangju had for me. I hungrily read all that I could lay a hand on. They had a collection of world classics in history, philosophy, and literature, like Plutarch's *Parallel Lives*, Stendhal's *Red and Black*, and many Chinese classics among other great works. These classics were introduced to me mainly through these collegians. They also played classical music and I got to know great western composers like Haydn, Mozart, Beethoven, Schubert, Brahms, and many others. The master also allowed me to attend night school near the American military base. I would stop the American soldiers and ask them how to pronounce certain words. One of my repeated encounters was showing a card with 'VEGETABLES' written on it and asking the American, "How do you pronounce this, please?" They would articulate the word as seriously as they could for this poor kid who was eager to learn English. My formal education might have stopped at the sixth grade, but I was absorbing new knowledge, in my own way, at a breathtaking rate. After the war, there were so many night schools everywhere that offered the war-torn nation alternative education for the dispersed and dispossessed. I took advantage of every opportunity to learn and, in a strange way, I was becoming a well-rounded student, free and creative, away from the stiff, ordered formal school systems.

One day, an unexpected visitor came to the house. It was my oldest half-brother who stopped on the way home to Gwangju. He had just been discharged from the army where he managed its boxing team for many years. As long as I could remember, he had always been in the army, through the war as a soldier and as a boxer thereafter. I was quite surprised at his visit, as I had not seen him since Father's funeral when he was on leave from the army to bury his father. He shared a short conversation with the master over tea and said something like he appreciated that his little (half) brother was being taken care of in this household. He told me later, when we were alone, that he was going back to Gwangju to become an active member of the local chapter of the Veterans' Association. The VA had become a politically influential group in Korea, since there were so many retired military men whose chapters were used for local politics. With his war experience and boxing background, he was already a celebrity of sorts. It was naturally expected that he would do well in the local VA organization. Of course, I had not known my older half-brother very well, as we had hardly spent time together as brothers and as family. Unlike my other half-brother who used to terrorize me with physical intimidation and food-stealing, this oldest half-brother was practically a stranger. It surprised me that he visited me at all. Equally surprising, it never occurred to me, when I saw my half-brother, to ask him to take me home and send me to school. The middle-school years were already passing me by and my age group was getting ready to go to high school. But the older brother I was looking at was altogether a stranger. For all practical purposes, we were not brothers at all.

My oldest half-brother was many years older than me and had spent a long career in the military as a boxing hero. It would have absolutely behooved me, and quite naturally so, to beg my big hero brother to take me home so I could go to school like my friends. Would he have taken me home with him if I had cried and begged? Because we had seldom lived together, and our blood being only half-thick, we had developed little brotherly affection. And because I had lived on the streets and alone for so long, fending for myself, I had forgotten that I had a brother who could save me. He came as my big brother. Yet, he was no real brother to me— just a stranger. So this great hero-brother came, had tea with the master, and said goodbye to his little brother who was working as a servant for this wealthy family. As far as I was concerned, I was alone in the world and was prepared to live there alone for the rest of my life. I remember watching my big brother walking slowly toward the train station (specialized in carrying military men to their destinations). When I saw him again many years later, it was a situation so dramatically different from what I had imagined. He had become an important figure in the Veterans Association's chapter in Gwangju as he had planned. But it was nothing like what I was thinking on that day near the train station. As I watched him walk toward the station on that day, however, I felt neither sadness nor anger when we said our goodbyes. Already, after two years or so on my own, my heart had hardened. This hero-brother was not my hero-brother, for my true heroes were in the great books and in the movies. So, my brother visited me as a stranger and left me as a stranger. It was the last time I saw anybody from my family for the next half a dozen years. Yet, there was nothing in my heart that I felt as my emotional reaction.

A year or so seemed to have passed by and my career as a houseboy suddenly came to an end. Their former houseboy, of high school age, was returning to this household to reclaim his old job after a year away from the city. At first, we were roomed together in what was my room and in what used to be his room. He was much older than me and could not have been a better role-model for boys of all ages. He was always studious, always disciplined, and always clean. He went to school every day, a rather great privilege as a houseboy, something I was never privy to nor dared to demand. He worked for the household only after school and on weekends. I was in awe of this Boy Scout par excellence.

It gradually dawned on me and everybody else that the two of us could not stay in the same household very long. One of the daily routines I was always looking forward to was the three meals a day I was served with the little girls. By then, I was a growing boy in need of much food. As my life with the Boy-Scout role-model was becoming visibly untenable, I was beginning to feel uncomfortable eating their food without enough work to do to justify it. But the master and the mistress said nothing as if they were waiting for us to make the move. Since I could not compete with this all-around golden boy, I was now staring at the possibility of the street as my next residency.

Finally, the situation had become quite obviously uncomfortable and I had to leave. The master called me into his room and told me what I had anticipated for some time. He said that since the household was not big enough for two houseboys, one had to go. Would I mind going to Inchon, the port city made famous for MacArthur's Inchon Landing during the war, for another job? He said one of his suppliers of ceramic insulators, with a small manufacturing outlet in Inchon, told him he could use a young fellow at his factory and household. In short, it was a houseboy position again, with a bit of hard labor added. Of course, I was not in a position to quibble. Shortly after the conversation with the master, I said goodbye once again to everyone, including the sweet girls who had been quite attached to me by then. I was on the way to Inchon, only about two hours' train ride from Seoul, but to an unknown destiny altogether. I had just reached the fourteenth year of my life.

IV. The Human Engine

My destination was actually a small rural village outside of Inchon that locals called *Sokbawi*, meaning 'Rock Hill.' Today, the village has become part of the City of Inchon, a thriving suburb, but at the time, Rock Hill was considered a distinct district, mostly poor and rural, apart from Inchon. Rock Hill was a small township scattered around a hill where mostly war refugees had built their dwellings helter-skelter, very likely without permission from the law. Most of the homesteaders had jobs elsewhere, so they commuted by bus or train every day. While their village was completely surrounded by rice paddies, there didn't seem to be any farmers among the residents there. In short, they lived surrounded by farms but they were refugees from elsewhere who had simply settled there and built their mud-and-straw-and-panel homes. This makeshift town was where I was destined to spend the next five years. I went there as a skinny boy of fourteen and left from there, after years of hard labor, as a fairly decent-looking youth of nineteen.

People in Sokbawi, or Rock Hill, who did not hold jobs somewhere else found employment at the huge ceramics factory that produced inexpensive everyday tableware like plates, bowls, and cups. Once in a while, its huge chimney spewed black smoke for two days, meaning its gigantic kiln was in operation, reaching up to over two thousand degrees in Fahrenheit. After the kiln cooled, the workers unloaded the baked wares which were then packed and shipped to their markets. The factory was always busy, dozens of potters' wheels constantly spinning and workers carrying the plaster molds that contained the wet clay wares to a room to dry. Those that were already dry were glazed with different colors and designs, to be baked in the next kiln firing. Their bells rang to announce the beginning and ending of each shift, and you could see the workers, shaking off their aprons full of clay dust, leaving the factory or coming into their shift.

The little cottage manufacturer at which I would spend the next five years of my life, a tiny one by comparison with the imposing ceramics factory next door, was located on the other side of the hilly divider with rice fields that were terraced from the top to the bottom. To cross the terraced rice fields, you had to use one of the thin walls, about a foot wide, that divided the terraces and also dammed up each terrace. If you missed your step as you walked on the thin wall, you would fall into the next terrace, about three-feet below, and endure the embarrassment of being covered with the black rice-paddy dirt. Intoxicated people occasionally fell into the muddy rice field, causing a good bit of laughter among the villagers. They still preferred to cross the divider walls of the terraced fields to avoid having go all the way up to the top of the hill and go around safely on a larger dirt road. During the winter while the fields lay fallow, snow would be collected deep against the banks and it was often difficult to tell where the snow ended and the dirt wall began.

The little factory of my new employment was built by cutting out a space on a small red hill so that the rear wall was simply the hill itself. Walls on the three open sides were patched up with makeshift straw mats and thin veneer panels, all hanging precariously. Many of these walls had been salvaged from the waste material collected from the American military bases whose trash provided a good deal of construction material for the poor Korean builders. The roof was covered with straw, giving the factory an appearance of a poor farm warehouse. Inside the factory was actually much more spacious than it promised from the outside. At the first glance, it was a miniature picture of the neighboring larger factory. But details betrayed the profound differences between the two. There were about half a dozen boys, mostly younger than me, and several adults engaged in all different facets of their functions. Unlike the larger factory next door, this small cottage industry produced ceramic insulators that were inserted between electric wires whenever two or more had to cross each other. If you saw a dangling bare-socket light bulb, that would likely be one of the ceramic insulators produced here. They were used in so many ways in electric wirings that required insulation around the residential houses and larger buildings that one hardly noticed them.

The boys were engaged in various steps, some forcing clay into the molds, some drying the wet insulators just taken out of the molds, and some kneading the clay into more pliable dough. One of the major differences between this cottage factory and the larger one next door was the absence of electric power. During the day, the sunlight through the windows provided enough lighting. At night, several large oil lamps burned brightly to illuminate the interior. For the five years I worked there, electric power never came to the factory. The one potter's wheel at this factory was powered by a human being, a boy about my age. The human engine had a sturdy industrial belt, about three feet in length, wrapped around the shaft of the wheel and was pulling it with his hands to make the shaft spin. He pulled one end of the belt with his right hand, while resisting it with his left hand, tightly around the shaft so that each pull produced the spin of the shaft to the right. The belt, tightly wrapped against the shaft, would spin the wheel continually at good speed as the human engine repeated the motion as if the potter's wheel was spinning powered by an electric motor. The worker, standing over the spinning potter's wheel, shaped the clay in the mold, each task taking about ten seconds. The spin from below (as the human engine had to sit down and pull the belt) and the mold-controller standing up worked in perfect coordination without wasting any of the hard pulling of the human engine. As it turned out, doing the human-engine job was considered the hardest work at the factory. Naturally, since I was to be the houseboy, not a regular employee, it was my destiny to be the designated human engine. Some of the employees were local boys from the neighborhood who worked there after school. The owner's younger brother, one of the two or three adult workers, was the master mold-maker and second in command.

Another tough job that was immediately assigned to me as the houseboy was transforming the hard-dried clay into supple dough that would fill the mold to produce a ceramic insulator. Since this little cottage industry bought its clay supply from the large factory next door, the condition in which the clay was delivered was always dry and hard. To reduce the cost, they would buy the cheaper dry clay and make it supple with human labor. They showed me the rudimentary technique of breaking and slicing the clay into thin pieces with a sharp army shovel that could also work as a pick and then soaking the sliced clay. When it was soaked enough, you pounded the softened clay slices with a large wooden mallet until the clay slices broke and stuck together enough to knead, which was the final step. The process was not only arduous, but it also left the worker completely caked all over the face and clothes with the splash from the clay while pounding it. Without proper clay ready to be used, there was no further progress at the production line. So, the pressure was enormous to keep wet clay-dough well supplied. Aside from being an all-around houseboy, my main functions at the factory consisted of being a human engine for the potter's wheel and clay-maker, both of which were exhausting and vital.

The owner, a refugee from North Korea, well-educated and wealthy at one time in his country before the family had escaped the Communist rule, had two younger brothers working at the factory. The youngest one, yet unmarried, was a bungling comedian who was always happy-go-lucky, who helped his owner-brother in many different roles, but mainly as a cheerleader. One of his bad habits consisted of choosing the more difficult word to use in his speech if he had a choice. The second brother, the master mold-maker, was a superb technician who used to be an army drill sergeant—serious and intelligent. All three brothers, formerly reputable and proud, were caught in this grinding business of producing ceramic insulators. The owner was constantly behind in payment to the local boys who worked there for part-time wages. There was another young man, smart and hardworking, who functioned as their official salesman. He would go to Seoul every morning, returning late in the day, a job everybody envied because he got to go to the capital city all the time. Several local young women, including the older girl of the landowner family who owned the factory ground, were eyeing the salesman for possible matrimony. Such was the totality of the crew at the factory in which I was their newest member.

There was actually a third job that fell on me that I did not welcome at all. It was fetching water for the second brother, the mold-maker, who lived in a one-room hut on top of the hill. As a houseboy for the owner, thus occupying the lowest rank in the establishment, it was my preordained task that I could not avoid. The master mold-maker's wife, who was constantly suffering from asthma, sent messenger after messenger for me to fetch water for her. Because of the work process that required my constant presence and labor, either as a human engine or as a clay-maker, I had to fetch the water only during my break. To fetch water, I had to balance the Chinese-style beam over my shoulders, with a bucket dangling on each end of the beam, and navigate down the hill to the nearest well that was dug where the corners of four adjacent rice paddies met. Most of those who came to fetch water were young women, some of whom would strike up a conversation with me now and then. There, I would wait for my turn, fill up the buckets, carry them back to the top of the hill, and pour the water into a tank in the master mold-maker's kitchen. Of course, the master mold-maker's wife was always grateful to me for supplying her the water and made sure her pretty little girl, about six, said 'thank you' to me for my labor. But I had a hard time hiding my dislike for this particular drudgery, for the simple reason that it broke the continuity of my work.

In a poor country like Korea, living was not easy. The affluent Korea, of Samsung, Hyundai, and LG, and the technological marvel that is modern Korea, was still decades away. Most people at this time were grinding out their daily survival as best as they could. At Rock Hill, having enough to eat was a daily struggle. The most common food that was our daily lot, aside from rice and kimchi, was the famed 'chicken and dumplings without chicken,' which Koreans called (as they still do) *'su-je-bi.'* The dish was made up of dumplings that were made up of flour and water. You spooned the dough into the boiling water mixed with soy sauce and whatever vegetables you could find. If you could add some real chicken, or even an egg or a potato in it, it was luxury. But you could always count on at least water and flour dumplings. Otherwise, any odds-and-ends remnants, vegetable or animal, were welcome as its ingredients. But for the hungry mouths, like mine all the time, anything that was not plain water was good food.

There was one particular character who often added nutrition to our meager diet. He was one of the villagers who worked with a group in Inchon, known to be an underground organization with shady criminal connections. He truly had a face—fearsome, red, and ugly—that only a mother could love. In his whole demeanor, he looked as if he had never left the cave where his human evolution had stopped. He was loud and boisterous but had many hilariously amusing gangster stories that kept the night workers highly entertained. The rumor was that he killed people, and we all tiptoed around him, making sure we did not offend him in anyway. This gangster would visit our factory, mostly at night, often bringing a live rabbit or a live chicken with him. Then we would strangle and skin the rabbit or strangle and pluck the chicken and boil it into decent rabbit stew or delicious chicken soup, which generally turned into a great feast for all. Naturally, we were happy to have him visit us. In spite of his fearsome reputation, he never harmed any of us or did anything hurtful to the wellbeing of the factory. He was like one of those characters in old stories where a monster everyone feared or loathed actually had a heart of gold.

The factory was also visited often by a young man, perhaps in his early twenties, very well-mannered and proper, quite a contrast to the gangster. He worked at Camp Market as a shoe-shiner for the American soldiers at the base. Camp Market, which is now reduced to a small-sized base today, was at the time a thriving U.S. military depot, located in a small city called Boopyung, about ten miles from Rock Hill. There, all the American military supplies arriving from the U.S. were distributed to the different bases in Korea. Working at an American base as a houseboy or a shoe-shiner had always been my dream job. A good part of my more immediate incentives to learn good English had to do with this dream job at an American base. I had detested the shoe-shining job when my stepmother demanded it, but doing the same work for Americans was different. The young man, my role-model, would describe his work for the American soldiers as something the factory boys, especially me, could only dream about. According to his descriptions, these American GIs were singularly generous, fair, and kind. Inspired by the success story of this young man, I decided to visit the city on my day off (which was rare) where the American base was located. Arriving on a bus, I was impressed by Boopyung, quite a metropolitan city, especially for a teenage factory worker from Rock Hill. Around Camp Market was a thriving military town with movie houses and coffee shops, and the usual businesses that catered to the American soldiers. Just hanging around the outside walls of the enormous American military base was awe-inspiring. Whatever might be going on inside the wall, just like the other side of the barbed wire in Yongsan with the little American girls, was the place for my most mystified imagination and fantasy. Surely behind the walls of the great American base existed the most beautiful homes with never-ending laughter inside and its streets all paved in gold. But the base was well protected by cinder-block walls, and the guards, both American and Korean, looked quite unforgiving for any possible intruder.

Later, I passed by a movie house which was showing a comic western called '*North to Alaska.*' It was a light action fair with John Wayne and Stewart Granger, who played two gold-diggers in Alaska, eventually vying for the affection of an appealing French woman played by Capucine. I enjoyed the movie but its aftermath, coming out to my miserable reality after a comic action story, was quite dreary. I was very unhappy with myself, especially with the dreamy wealth and happiness inside the American base that I could only imagine. For solace, I walked into a coffee shop nearby and ordered some sweet coffee. I hadn't sat there very long at the coffee shop when the coffee shop owner/server walked over to me and told me to leave. I was quite surprised at this sudden eviction notice.

"Leave? Why?" I asked, incredulous.

"Your face," he said.

"What about my face?" I asked, still incredulous.

"Your face looks very miserable," he said matter-of-factly. "It's giving other customers a very bad impression," the owner said. He was merely protecting his business interest.

Although I had been considered a relatively good-looking boy (Actually, some called me downright handsome.), this declaration from the coffee-shop owner evoked no particular resistance from me. I didn't argue. It was a miserable day off anyway. It didn't hurt my feelings at all, as I had never thought of myself as either miserable-looking or particularly handsome. I obeyed the owner's order and left the coffee shop peaceably and returned home by bus. I took solace that in the history of humanity, I might have been the only person ever evicted from a coffee-shop because of the 'miserable' look of my face. The result of my excursion to Boopyung was that America loomed ever more fantastic and my present life ever more dispiriting.

During the winter, the most difficult part of the ceramic production had to do with drying the clay products after they were molded. Since the sun outside was scarce and weak, we had to use stoves with what they then called nineteen-hole coal briquettes. You would just stack a fresh briquette on top of a waning one, each briquette lasting close to half a day, and continue this process for good heat for twenty-four hours a day. One of the problems with this, often deadly all over Korea, was that these nineteen-hole briquettes produced silent but lethal carbon monoxide when they burned. If inhaled in enough quantity, the gas would kill a person; sometimes an entire family would fall victim to carbon monoxide poisoning. Most Koreans used this method to heat their homes in the winter, and fatalities were reported daily from its toxic effects. When we used the coal to dry the insulators, everyone made sure that the ventilation was sufficient and everyone watched out for symptoms in one another. (At the time, close to 80% of Korean households used the briquettes. Today, it is reduced to less than 2%, as they have switched to oil, gas, and electricity. But the briquettes are now used as a common instrument of suicide among the Koreans.)

One particular cold day, I was sitting near the stove and inhaling a good bit of its carbon monoxide. It was early in the morning and I had worked through the night. I had fallen asleep near the stove, obviously too close to its toxic carbon monoxide, which was odorless. An adult shook me awake and told me to go home to bed. I shared a room with several others at the top of the hill in a mud-and-straw house, which meant I walked on one of the thin walls to cross the terraced fields to get to the other side as a shortcut. After being awakened, I stood up and walked out of the building and started toward the terraced wall covered with deep snow. I took several steps on the terrace wall and was overcome by the carbon monoxide I had unknowingly inhaled. I staggered and helplessly fell off the thin footpath and into the deep snow, which had accumulated toward the bank of the next terrace. I am not sure how long a youth can survive buried in snow on a freezing day. I was consciously aware that I had fallen down into the pile of snow but I was powerless to move. I don't recall how long I had to lay in the snow. It was very early in the morning and, quite fortunately, a few people were already up and about, including some who were crossing the terraces to go to the bus or train station. One of them spotted the dark clump in the snow. He pulled me out and shouted for help. The neighborhood was instantly alerted. In no time, somebody poured a bowl full of *kimchi* juice into my mouth, which, because of its peculiar ingredients, woke me up immediately, like magic. Apparently, it was well known as a remedy for the not-so-rare carbon monoxide poisoning. They let me sleep it off for most of the day and I returned to work later. This was the first time that I had actually experienced near death and providence saved me. Also, it was the last time that I had a brush with death as a laboring teenager in the rough-and-tumble era of post-war Korea.

Because our factory had no kiln of its own, the owner often rented a corner of the kiln space at the bigger factory for our small wares. Sometimes, the mutual schedules didn't meet and we had to carry our insulators to be baked at kilns in other larger factories. On those days, we would box the all-dried and glazed products carefully in apple boxes, with rice husks filling the spaces between them so that they would not scrape off each other's glaze. Often, the distances involved miles, and we would carry the boxes on our backs, all according to our own physical abilities, including the owner himself, and make our trek in a single file. This was literally and figuratively back-breaking work. We would rest once in a while and eat an apple or two that the owner brought with him for our morale and nutrition. If there was any providential reward from such labor, it was that I was becoming stronger, especially from the human engine part that strengthened my torso and heart muscles.

One day, the owner brought to the factory a gasoline-powered engine the size of a small briefcase. It looked shiny and impressive in shimmering black when it was taken out of a box. All the factory workers, and some neighbors, came to see this great advancement in modern technology. This new machine symbolized the monumental transition for this factory, from pre-modern to modern, in its development. I was particularly delighted that this new machine was going to relieve me of my infernal work as a human engine. We all surrounded the new technological marvel with heightened expectations. But to our surprise and disappointment, when the owner, and his know-it-all younger brother, poured gasoline into it and started it, it belched black smoke and, after a very irregular turn or two, sputtered into silence. They read the manual and tried it again and again, but the shiny engine refused to cooperate. It sputtered and died each time. Very puzzled, the performers and the spectators both decided that the gasoline-powered engine was useless. I was bitterly disappointed that I had to go back to my human engine work. The machine was put away and after a while it was forgotten, until one day, to my great surprise, my master from Yongsan, where I had been a houseboy, visited our factory to check on an especially expensive set of insulators that he had ordered that were late in delivery. He asked me how I was doing (I had grown up somewhat by then.), and after one thing or another, the conversation drifted to the failed gasoline-operated engine. The master's eyes lit up.

"I can fix it. Bring it out," he said, to everyone's surprise. "I used to fix those engines all the time."

They fetched the engine and brought it to my former master. He checked and tinkered with the machine this way and that for a minute or so and, declaring that it was now working perfectly, turned it on. The machine hummed beautifully. I felt a sense of pride. He used to be my master and I was very proud that I had once been his houseboy. The know-it-all youngest brother was quite embarrassed but was happy that it was now in good working order! The engine replaced me as the turner of the potter's wheel for a while. But due to its abuse, it did not last very long. I continued to be their more reliable human engine.

Life was harsh at the insulator factory. But as I became more of a part of the factory and the village, I managed to adjust my time and work so that I could attend night school in Inchon. Again, it was one of those charity schools with no formal accreditation. But such schools were many in post-war Korea with a high concentration of people who were eager for education. I would ride a bus to the city, take the classes I wanted, mostly English and other subjects, including typing, and return home late at night. Sometimes, I would miss the last bus and would have to walk miles back to Rock Hill. I was gaining height and weight, as I was now growing up, and my knowledge was growing too. The local boys who worked at the factory were always impressed with my vast knowledge about everything and called me 'Baksa-nim,' meaning 'Great Doctor of Knowledge.'

Except for the uncertainty of my future, I was getting into the rhythm of life in this strange situation. As my English ability began to impress the villagers, I was asked to tutor English for one of the kids, a chubby rosy-cheeked boy, about ten. While my employment status was still quite low-brow, this tutoring position suddenly elevated me in the eyes of my fellow workers. The boy had two older twin sisters in their early twenties and these older women took a shining to me. After English lessons, I was invited to take long walks with one of them. We engaged in deep conversations on all sorts of topics, and, becoming aware of the pleasure of female companionship, I thoroughly enjoyed these long walks. I had dropped my Gwangju accent a long time ago, acquiring the standard Seoul dialect, and had forgotten all about my stepmother and half-brothers. For years, I was so busy surviving that I seldom thought about my past. I had never written them and was sure they cared not if I lived or died.

One day, an announcement was made by the owner. He had accidentally run into an old friend from North Korea who offered him a job as the manager of a hotel in Seoul that the friend owned. In the meantime, he had sold the factory to a friend who would be taking over the operation soon. The new owner and his beautiful wife (It was whispered that his first wife had committed suicide.) came to Rock Hill on their inspection trip. His new beautiful wife had been a nurse and she would offer free medical care to the employees and villagers. The new owner had some reserve capital, unlike the always-scraping-by former owner, and decided to build a kiln of his own and build a house next to the kiln and factory. The kiln was significant as a sign of independence from the bigger factories whose kiln space always had to be begged. Some sense of regularity and stability, if not prosperity, came to the always unpredictable factory operation. The factory itself had a facelift and improved its look after extensive remodeling.

Significantly enough, a close friend of the new owner and his wife, two very friendly people, visited us at the factory site. This was significant for me in particular because this friend worked as a bartender at Camp Red Cloud, an American military base north of Seoul—my eternal dream place! A bartender at the American military base! I remembered how I had envied the shoe-shiner at Camp Market. But this man was working at an American base as a bartender! My most-dreamed-of career dream had intensified further after my Camp Market debacle. The owner's friend carried on a conversation in English with me, profusely using the 'f-ing' word, which impressed me profoundly. Anyone who could use the f-ing word so profusely was a great English speaker in my book. He was equally impressed that I spoke English and that I had the houseboy experience. Could he please help me get a job at Red Cloud? After my urgent plea, he agreed to help me. First, he would get a job-application form, all in English, from the camp and would send it to me. I could then fill it out and bring it back to Red Cloud and submit it.

I eventually received the application form and filled it out very carefully. The very next day, I took a day off and rode the bus, a two-hour ride, to Camp Red Cloud. The camp, pretty much like Camp Market and all other American military bases in Korea, had the distinct, long cinder block walls whose top was enforced with barbed wire, with the signs, in both English and Korean, warning people to keep out. It must have been job-application day. There was a long line of people alongside the wall that stretched from the main entrance. Looking at the long line of people, potentially my competitors, my confidence sagged. I didn't feel very confident that something good was going to happen to me. There were just too many people, although few were my age. I walked back to the end of the line and waited. The line moved relatively fast, and in no time I was face-to-face with what I considered a Hawaiian-looking American, fat and swarthy, who was standing there behind a podium. I moved up to him.

"Next," he said, looking at me. I handed him my precious application form. "Thank you. We will call you if we need you," he said. He gave me no chance to show off my English.

He then collected my application and added it to the stack that he had already collected from the others. That was it? When I stood there, so lost and not knowing what to do next, he motioned to go on, and out. I was devastated! Was this all? My dream of finding a houseboy job at an American base was so cruelly broken! I was just one little paper, among many papers! I had come all the way from Inchon to submit the precious application form to the United States military base for a job. I spoke English and had houseboy experience, but all for naught! I was at the end of the line, and that was it. I am sure I rode the bus home, but with such a destroyed heart that I have no clear recollection of how I got home. I only remember the bus ride, very vaguely at that. My human engine and clay-busting life had to continue for quite a while longer.

I now became seventeen years old, eligible to join the navy. This ambition was prompted by the new mistress's brother who was just discharged from the navy. He said the navy was a good career and for a smart kid like me, there were many opportunities. The only trouble was that entrance into the navy required a minimum middle-school education, which I didn't have. The retired navy man was resourceful. He said not to worry. He would fix one for me. In no time, he brought me an official-looking document that said I had a middle-school education. For good measure, he wrote a nice reference letter on my behalf, swearing that I was not a Communist and I had no relatives who were Communists. None of my acquaintances was a Communist. The application package was accepted and a date was set for my physical.

The physical took place at a small school in a nearby city. Several dozen young men wearing only their undershorts were lining up here and there to get their physical. Obviously, they were all future navy men. I went through several doctors and examiners. Everything seemed to go all right, and then I came to the dental section. A young fellow with a dental mirror examined my teeth and hollered, "Cavity present. Disqualified!"

"What?" I didn't understand what he had just hollered and ask him to repeat it, which he did. I had a cavity? Apparently, Koreans had extraordinarily healthy teeth and one cavity was going to disqualify me from the navy! After all the trouble of getting ready for this application, I was rejected from the navy because of one lone cavity! Once again, I was so devastated and dejected at the rejection that I do not recall how I returned home after the disqualification. Instead of riding the great waves of the seven seas, my human engine and clay busting life awaited me for two more years. But, of course, in this rejected navy application, it was a call from providence. If I had passed my physical and joined the navy, my adult story would have been quite different.

Even under the new ownership and management, my life hardly changed, except that I was growing up fast. And the most significant event in my life took place about this time—I lost my virginity! It took place inside the new kiln, built by the new owner, which was finally operational. After each firing, for about three days or so, the kiln, warm and cozy, remained a wonderful place to sleep on cool nights. It happened one night with the house maid, a few years older than me, who came to my room and motioned me to come out. I followed her out and she led me to the kiln, which was still warm from the last firing. There were floor mats here and there on which workers had slept when the kiln was warmer. At that time in the kiln, we were the only people and we lay on one of the mats for a while. She was scheduled to go home the next day to live with her sister in another city, and she talked about her sister. Then it happened and, in some uncertainty and tenderness, I bade farewell to my boyhood in the kiln that night. The next day, the maid said goodbye to the new mistress and everybody else but hardly said anything to me. I never saw my first love again.

Days and months passed and something was stirring all over Korea. People in business suits, seldom seen in our part of the town, were seen all over the rice fields. They would stand here and there and point to this and that, nodding and discussing. The rumor was that they were the new land speculators who were buying all the farmlands to build huge apartments. To confirm these rumors, the present owner and his wife announced one day that they were selling their land and property too. And just like that, the factory closed. The place where I had worked as the human engine and clay buster for close to five years, where I had grown from a boy to an almost-young man, losing my virginity, closed without fanfare. The owner and his wife gave me the keys to the buildings, trusting me as the caretaker until the new owner came to claim the land and property. The new owner had nothing to do with ceramic insulators, as they had purchased the place for its land value. Just like that, it was all empty and silent now. I would stay there in the empty house and silent factory until the new owner came.

One of the last employees, a boy two years younger than me, named Tai, who had joined the factory not too long ago, came to the house to console me. He and I had become good friends especially because his family had an old Japanese-made phonograph, with two Viennese waltz records. It was still in good condition. We enjoyed playing the phonograph until we ran out of the metal needles that had come with it. Poor Tai dropped out of school because he had developed a stomach ulcer at a young age, which caused him to rub his stomach all the time. Always eager to learn new things to make up for the school he was not part of, he looked up to me as his big brother and mentor, although my own schooling had been just as short. Tai and I decided to make an inventory of what was left on the premises to see if there was anything we could salvage. When we inspected the warehouse that had been built by the new owner when he was upgrading the factory, we found that there was a stack of crates full of ceramic insulators in them! We were quite shocked with what we had discovered—a treasure trove of things we had never been told about. After all, since the old owner had left and the new one had not come yet, this was open season on the owners. In between the two, it was no man's land and everything belonged to us, the finders, the caretakers! Facing this very difficult moral choice, we examined our conscience briefly and decided that our existential considerations overrode all other moral issues.

Following some serious tactical discussions, we decided to test the field. To make sure it was safe from prying eyes, we waited until dark before we carried a box of insulators out and rode the bus to Inchon. Not too far from the bus terminal was a retail market where such electric items were sold individually. We took the box to one of the stores and asked the man if he wanted to buy some ceramic insulators. The man, after inspecting the items, agreed and paid us what we thought was a handsome amount. Tai and I could not believe our luck. We ate a very nice dinner and went to see a movie and came home late at night. A few days later, our criminal excitement had died down and our feeling of guilt had also subsided. And, of course, hunger for good food returned too. We decided to try just one more box. We repeated our operation, riding the bus to Inchon and collecting our money from the same storeowner. Great dinner and a movie followed. After the second time, we became more daring. We did it virtually every night—great dinner and a movie, great dinner and a movie. Life was great, and soon there were no more boxes left. Luckily for us, the new owner finally showed up and took the keys and declared my services done.

Here it was, in Rock Hill, a chapter in my life had come to an end. The factory where I worked for five years of hard labor had closed. But by some strange quirk of fate, another chapter opened up. The energetic salesman, the romantic target of all the village girls, continued to stay in the sales business for electric insulators even after the factory closed. He visited the factory one day, for the purpose of talking to me, and told me that he needed somebody to help with the new store that he had just opened near Seoul Train Station. Would I come to Seoul and join him? I was thrilled.

It was about this time of my life that I was sensing something only vaguely but discernable enough for me to be aware of. Whenever I was in trouble, or was at the end of my rope, so to speak, there seemed to be something, someone, who came forward to help me. This was only a vague notion, a notion that I was always protected and helped by some indescribable force of providence. Decades later, when I converted to Catholicism, this providential force guiding my life was one of the main reasons for my conversion. There was always something, a mystical, shadowy power, from the daily details to the grand intellectual enterprises, that was hovering over me.

But practical matters always loomed first. Even as I and my friend Tai were enjoying the nightly pleasures of selling pilfered insulators, I had been aware that something significant was taking place in my life. I was losing my employment soon, and had no idea where I would go after that. I was also aware that I was getting close to nineteen years of age. Was I tall enough for my age? What was my future going to be? I had no education pedigree, no connection, and no family! At least, the salesman's offer was a job, and I would not have to be on the street for a while. But deep down in my thinking, I was quite worried about what my future would bring. In many ways, it seemed hopeless and dark. I could not imagine anything would brighten my life. As I was getting ready to go to Seoul to work for the salesman, these questions cast a shadow in my mind that was full of anxiety, fear, and uncertainty. I was cast out on the street nearly eight years ago and I was not sure what kind of a human being I had become in the ensuing years. After all, I was a laborer. I had not lived with family and had not received any formal education the whole time. I found myself asking: *What have I become?*

Looking back, the five years I spent at the factory were good years in which I earned a living with honest labor. I came out a reasonably wholesome youth, with no particular health issues or injuries. By attending the night schools religiously, I had acquired much academic knowledge, although without proper credits, and my English was quite good in both writing and speaking by then. I even took a college entrance exam on a lark and passed so that I could say I was qualified to enter college if the chance ever came. My love of reading had continued and by the time I was leaving Rock Hill, I had read most of the world classics. Stendhal's *Julien Sorel* and Goethe's *Werther* had become my melancholic heroes who were dealt a bad hand by fate. Later, my new American hero, Shane, overtook the gloomy European ones with a brighter and more naturalistic brand of heroism and idealism. For economic reasons more than anything, I never took to drinking or smoking, and my entire life I was free of these pesky habits. Even at UCLA as a graduate student years later, I never touched pot, which was highly unusual. On the flip side of such a superficially wholesome youth was the deep, dark price I was paying as a person whose whole focus of survival was on himself and himself alone. In short, I had become quite incapable of normal emotions as a human being. I was strong and disciplined, not easily given to sentimentality. But I had also become quite unsympathetic to human weaknesses and intellectual stupidity. By the time I left Rock Hill, I was a jumble of extremes: strong beliefs in justice and perfection so easily mixed with the desire to sin and compromise if it served my own ends. My future depended thus on what my ends would be and how providence would stack up to shape, guide, or obstruct these ends. There was not a single thing I could do, with my own will and decision alone, for I had no useful or powerful resources on my side. Like a little boat in the rough sea, my whole fate depended on what providence would bring me—a calm sea or a turbulent storm. With no formal education, no family, and no particular skill, my fate was wholly in the hands of providence.

The villagers in Rock Hill, mostly refugees from the war, were sweet people, hardworking and untainted by the later onrush of capitalism and individualism that were ordained for Korea. As I knew them and lived among them, they were morally superior to any group of people I had known. The five years among them were rough times, harsh and relentless, always one foot near disasters. But I was mostly safe and reasonably protected, even surviving the carbon monoxide poisoning. I could have turned into a rough and tumble youth of extreme savagery and boorishness. But for the most part during those years in Rock Hill, I had kept my idealism and my basic lifelong yearning for a just world. When I look back from retirement, in Massachusetts, I can say that most of my character traits, good and bad, were formed during those five hard years in Rock Hill. The rest were mere details. Now, finding a new job as a storekeeper in Seoul, I was still facing an unknown chapter in my young life. At nineteen, my childhood was finally coming to an end. So were the days of my hard labor.

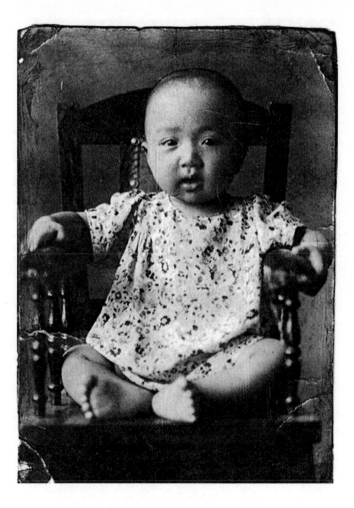

When I was 100 days old

The picture sent to the newspaper.

Happy horse rider, about 2.

With my sweet half-brother

My mother before marriage

A studio photo of my mother

As a houseboy, perhaps 13, with a college mentor

The Human Engine, at 17

At 19, just before finding my family

Unhappy nephew, with a new uncle

Now retired, with wife, Terry

V. Coming Home

The store that the salesman had opened, about two blocks away from Seoul train station, was hardly a store. The 'store' had more empty space than used. The mostly barren store had about a dozen electric insulators, many of which I had a hand in making at the factory. They were on display on a makeshift wooden structure with several layers. (At this time, Korea, later famed for its workmanship rivaling Japan's in quality, had virtually everything in makeshift fashion, haphazard and helter-skelter.) There was at least one foot of space between the articles. Indifferent passersby would cast a quick glance only because it occupied a store space on a very busy street. Other than that, both the store and the storekeeper were *persona non grata*. Nobody ever stopped by there during the few months I worked as a storekeeper, either out of curiosity or in earnest business interest. I never understood the real purpose of the store being there. However, the very location of the store was important, as it was only one or two blocks from Korea's largest train station. As passengers were disgorged from the trains hourly and daily, most of them had only two directions to go: either going left to go toward the downtown (passing by a small hotel where my former employer was the manager) or right toward the Han River (of my teary lunchbox encounter). Because the number of travelers coming from the south was considerable, the thought came to me that it was inevitable that I would run into someone sooner or later who might recognize me. But I thought about such a possibility only in retrospect. At the time, watching the throng of people coming and going at the train station, this possibility had no particular significance.

In this uncertain time of my life and in the history of Korea, a very significant event occurred that would affect both my little life and the whole nation of Korea. I witnessed the famous May 16, 1961 military takeover of Korea by high-ranking army officers led by General Park Chung Hee. The citizens awoke on that day hearing the sound of gunfire from the direction of the Han River. Within an hour, the citizens of Seoul were seeing army tanks all over their capital city. People poured out wanting to know what was going on. Our store was only a few blocks away from Seoul's City Hall, and just a few more blocks from the Blue House, the president's office building, where the main events seemed to be taking place. I actually ventured out to city Hall myself. Soldiers standing nearby their tanks were handing out pamphlets which announced that the military junta was taking over the government from the prime minister, his cabinet and the national assembly (equivalent to the U.S. Congress). The news of this shocking event continued throughout the day. It announced that the prime minster and his cabinet were under arrest, basically unharmed, the national assembly dissolved, all mayors and provincial governors dismissed and replaced by military officers. The supreme power of Korea was now vested in the hands of a junta made up of generals. They promised to reform corrupt Korea and push it into the modern world. To assure the American Military stationed in Korea that this wasn't some Communist plot, and deter it from interfering, the junta promised to maintain a strong alliance with the U.S. against the Communists up north. Soon, Park was invited to the White House for a meeting with President Kennedy, which legitimated the takeover as *fait accompli*. Coup d'etat. Government Takeover. Industrialization. These were heady developments for hitherto largely backward Korean society at large. But for me, my life still consisted of consuming the three daily meals and surviving the day.

The subsequent unfolding of the military coup on the front pages of the newspapers filled with exciting news and commentaries. Exciting and unprecedented as the historical development was, concerning the rapid change in Korea that it would bring about, it meant nothing at that little dusty shop near the train station. My life remained totally unaffected by the earth-shaking goings-on. We later heard that some soldiers guarding the bridge on the Han had been killed by the junta tanks. Yet, even this bloodshed had so little to do with me or the shop. Of course, I was totally wrong about this. If I had been endowed with any prophetic ability, I would have known how significant this military coup would have portended to affect the nation of Korea and its economic fame and my little, at the time totally insignificant personal, life.

The salesman-owner would stop by the shop once a day or so, inquiring on the general conditions of his store. Most of the time, there was nothing to report and he didn't seem to be too concerned about the progress, or lack thereof. But before he hurried off to his daily business, whose nature I never understood, he would hand me what amounted to a few dollars for my daily sustenance. What he gave me daily was exactly what I needed for three meals, the identical meals three times a day. I was a fast-growing youth of nineteen years, and what the skimpy vegetarian meals supplied me, with little or no protein at all in them, made me hungry again within an hour. Every day, my greatest preoccupation was running to my favorite tent restaurant just one block away from the back of the store where hungry laborers would congregate for cheap meals. Each one of these tent restaurants, forming a long row of individual eateries, offered a slightly different menu for its own individuality. Customers, the poor workers from around the area in various capacities, including myself, sat at the chairs along the L-shaped table provided at each establishment to eat their meals. Late at night, when there were no more customers, the restaurant's owner-operators would simply cover up their businesses and go home. Often, these movable tent restaurants would be taken down, folded up, and hauled to a new location quite easily if the situation required it.

There was one particular tent that served what they called 'military stew,' or in popular jargon, 'pig's stew,' with intoxicating smells of meats in the stew. The military stew, boiling in a huge cauldron constantly stirred by the server, was made up of the scraps discarded from the American military bases. The common rumor that always swirled around this particular food source was that the stew contained many inedible objects like cigarette butts and rotten eggs. It was always considered cheaper and more nutritious than the traditional, mostly vegetarian Korean meals served in tent establishments, euphemistically called 'covered wagons.' The American stew with abundant meat remnants in it was a strong temptation to the poor hungry souls like me. In spite of the strong temptations from my forever-demanding stomach, however, I never touched the American Military stew. One of the greatest weaknesses, my pride, always prevailed over the demands of my hungry stomach. (Today, this origin of the 'military stew' has morphed into a respectable dish called 'budae-jigae,' literally meaning 'military stew,' with similar ingredients, minus cigarette butts and rotten eggs. I doubt any modern customers who favor this respectable dish know that its genesis is in the throwaway scraps from the U.S Military's food trash.)

Years later, Korea became the only third-world nation, one of the poorest, if not the poorest, in the world, that moved to the threshold of an 'advanced' nation. This is a remarkable development that verges on a 'miracle,' as it is often called, because third-world nations, mostly former colonies, tend to remain forever third-world. Many questions have been raised and discussions held (to which I contributed years later with my own book, *Marching Orders*). One analysis that has never been done is the role of the 'trash' from the American military bases stationed in Korea and how it affected Korea's economic development. Indeed, beginning with the end of World War II, America's wastefulness had become prodigious. With war's end, arms' productions switched to consumer goods.

Automobiles, washing machines, and refrigerators, among other consumer goods, replaced guns and bombers. The American consumers, hitherto suppressed by the Great Depression and World War II, and thus free of debt, went all out with a vengeance to consume and consume to their hearts' content. Indeed, one of the first casual social comments from an American that has remained in my mind to this day was by a janitor who muttered to himself, "We sure waste a lot in this country."

This culture of wasting had spilled into the U.S. Military Establishment, especially the bases that were stationed in post-war Korea. The 'trash,' in food and day-to-day material consumption in the American Military became a great cottage industry in Korea. Koreans recycled everything that the American Military threw away. Even the empty Coca-Cola cans were flattened and turned into building materials that became panels for housing construction. Of course, to the poor Koreans, America's profligate waste merely added to the myth of a nation whose streets were paved in gold. For the Koreans, this gold was in America's trash also. It was rumored that the man who was licensed to handle U.S. Military trash was amassing a fortune, enough to create a massive industrial giant later known as 'Hyundai Motors.' The food trash that had turned into the tempting 'military stew' was only the visible component of America's colossally wasteful culture and economy. History says Korea's famed economic development emerged, in part, from the trash that Americans were throwing away. Indeed, one man's trash is another man's treasure.

In 1961, I was still in poor Korea, keeping the store for three meals a day. The new occupation at the store kept me alive but not much else. All of my income was spent in supplying my three meals a day. There was not a penny left from that income and this economic fact was creating a serious living crisis for me. The clothes that I had acquired at the factory in Rock Hill were now critically showing their age in wear and tear. But given the fact that my present employment was producing no discernable profits for my employer, I could hardly ask for a raise for clothes. It was a slow-burning crisis, slowly unraveling one thread a day, nothing radical but surely headed in the wrong direction. Sooner or later, the unraveling would have me naked.

As it seems to have happened so many times in my life, however, something occurred to spur a dramatic change in my life's direction. Whenever I thought I had come to the end of my rope, something decisive would break out. It was not just something; it was actually made up of *two somethings*, one after the other, a sort of good news and bad news, except that the bad news came first. The bad news was that the salesman-owner's baby brother, about my age who got tired of his farm life, decided to join his successful salesman brother in the fabled capital, except that the successful salesman-brother didn't seem very successful, nor was the capital city as fabulous as it was talked about among country folks. But to the hitherto farm boy, his brother was a great man of success and the capital city was a fabulous metropolis of excitement. Naturally, the farm boy decided to stay in Seoul with his hero-brother. The practical result of this unexpected family reunion was that there were now two, not one, largely useless storekeepers. Of the two, I was slightly more 'useless,' more dispensable, than the bloodline employee. Blood was obviously thicker than water or air, or even the memory of our struggle together in Rock Hill. This was quite reminiscent of my life as a houseboy in Yongsan where I was competed out of my job by a golden-boy alternative in a similar situation. In this tenuous position, I envied the farm boy's good fortune of having a brother like the salesman.

This quite uncomfortable situation did not last very long, because the second event, the 'good news,' followed the first one soon. I got my own hero-brother! One of the passengers who arrived on the train one day was one of my older half-brother's acquaintances, who somehow recognized me as he passed by the store. It was actually the first time that I had met anyone from home in close to ten years. I recalled the time that my half-brother had visited me on the way home from the army when I was a houseboy in Yongsan, which tested my heart with indifference and sorrow. The man told me that this ex-boxer-and-bouncer half-brother of mine was doing exceedingly well in Gwangju, where he was now a high-ranking official in the Veterans' Association. No doubt, my half-brother had put his boxer's fame and bouncer's frame to good use. He had instantly noticed that my situation in Seoul was not a happy one and, upon returning to Gwangju, told my half-brother about his little brother surviving by the skin of his teeth. The man returned to Seoul in no time and told me the most wonderful news I had ever heard in my life; my successful half-brother wanted me to come home and he would send me to college! Oh, what justice in heaven! I was now going back home to go to college, and my life time of misery and suffering was now coming to an end! My half-brother wanted me to come home so that I could go to college, like all of my friends and classmates! I wanted to shout to the world that now I had a family that wanted me to come home. Oh, how wonderful those words were! *My family wants me to come home and they would send me to college!* My days of suffering and my nights of misery were no more, and I would forget all those days and nights, as I would go to college like all of my friends! It was the beginning of the summer, hot and humid, and it was going to be the most beautiful summer of my life!

When I told the storeowner and his little brother the good news, they were not entirely unhappy to see me go, given the developing circumstance. The only problem that emerged from our celebration was that I didn't have any decent pants to wear for my homecoming. After ten years of exile, I didn't want to go home in my tattered pants. I was too ashamed. This problem was solved by the generosity of the salesman's little brother, who was about my height. He would loan me a pair of his trousers and I would send them back to him after my triumphant homecoming. Surely, my now-well-to-do hero-brother would buy me an entirely new wardrobe. In no time, I said goodbye to my hitherto benefactor and rode the train home. It was nothing like the last train ride where, after failing to sell the stolen bicycle, I had paid for the ticket with a hard slap in the face. This time, I was going home like a conquering hero, and no face-slapping because the salesman-employer paid for the ticket. After all, I had not become a pickpocket, I had not become crippled by industrial injuries, and I had become a decent scholar, ready for college in spite of my ten years of hard labor at factories. The long days of lonely brooding, and the longer nights of solitary lamentation, were over and now I could meet and talk to my former classmates to announce my good fortune. I arrived in Gwangju Train Station that afternoon and found my stepmother's new house not too far from the print-shop building.

My stepmother's finances must have diminished some since I last saw her. Their new house was much smaller than the home from which I was expelled ten years prior, although they still had a nice yard full of flowers and plants. Two women, my stepmother and my half-brother's live-in companion, a pretty woman of about late thirties who used to be a hairdresser, welcomed me home. The memory of my ordeal with the stepmother was still vivid, kept alive in my nightmares. But I was happy to be home and feeling welcomed into the family again. Under the celebratory circumstances of my homecoming, it was natural for this hitherto lonely boy to feel generous and forgiving toward his former tormentor. After nearly a decade of lone existence with no close family member anywhere, being with a family at home was a wonderful relief of tenderness. My hardened heart relaxed and truly rejoiced in its homecoming. They told me that my half-brother, busy at the Veterans' Association office, would be home shortly. My other half-brother, who used to take part of my rice by force, was already in the military for his mandatory service, but following in his older brother's footsteps, he was assigned to a boxing unit, stationed not too far from home so that he would be coming home to see me during the weekend. The two women and the homecoming boy were sitting around, drinking tea and eating cake, waiting for the man of the hour, my successful hero-brother, who made the whole happy occasion possible.

As we sat and talked, the summer night was drawing to darkness and my half-brother still did not come home. My stepmother said to her live-in daughter-in-law, "Doesn't he know his little brother is coming home today?"

My half-brother's live-in companion replied, "Of course, he does. Let me call the office again." The house did not have a phone and she went out somewhere to use a public telephone. She returned a few minutes later. There was a puzzled look on her face, and she said, "Nobody answered the phone at the office." We were unconcerned, just assuming that my half-brother, important and likely to be busy, had been held up somewhere on business. The sense of puzzlement soon changed to a sense of some concern, still vague and undefined. The night was getting pitch-dark and the bare light bulb that shone toward the garden was attracting all sorts of bugs and flies. We were sitting on the wooden platform placed between the house and the garden, still enjoying our reunion and conversations. Ten years was a long time and there was a lot to catch up on.

Then, a man knocked on the gate and the two women quickly recognized him as one of the clerks at the Veterans' Association. There was a sense of oddity immediately affecting all of us.

"Big brother has been arrested," he said forlornly. 'Big brother' was their honorific term of endearment for someone they respected but who was not officially higher-ranked. The two women reacted with puzzle, surprise, and shock. "Why? By whom?" they asked simultaneously.

That night, after the man left, and many days thereafter, this is what I pieced together. Over the years, the Veterans' Association in Korea was embroiled in political struggle for control. Because virtually all men in Korea served in the conscription military, and its powerful political influence-peddling was wide and deep, the VA local chapters in major cities were constantly in conflict with one another in intrigue and for power. Different chapters aligned themselves with certain political factions and their alignment shifted according to the fortunes of power, influence, and often money. In Gwangju, two factions of the VA chapter, Faction-A and Faction-B, were vying for control under the leadership of two retired colonels. Often, they fought politically with elections and what not, but more often, they fought physically, involving thuggery and violence like gangsters. My half-brother, with his background as a boxer and a bouncer, became a valuable member for Faction-A, led by a retired colonel who was also a lawyer. By using all sorts of methods, some legal and some illegal, and largely customary, Faction-A scored the victory and took control of the VA chapter in the city. The leader of Faction-B, defeated and bitter, swore revenge. Then the military coup of May 16, the event that I witnessed myself in Seoul and thought nothing of, altered everything. The supreme junta, after dismissing all the elected officials in cities and provinces, appointed the leader of Faction-B as the new commander of the city district under martial law. The new commander naturally put all his political enemies under arrest as one of his first official acts. My half-brother, on that memorable day when his little half-brother was coming home, so full of hope and pride, was one of the men arrested. It bore ill because my half-brother's role in securing the victory for Faction-A had been quite considerable and the future seemed predictably dark. The family spent the night in awful uncertainty and in evil foreshadowing. My own life, the reason for the celebratory family festivity and reunion, suddenly diminished to the insignificant. The little brother from Seoul who came home triumphantly was now indeed *little*, and even the 'brother' part was doubtful under the sudden shift of our fortunes. It was indeed amazing how quickly the fortunes of a little brother who had to depend on the larger forces of luck could change from everything to nothing.

The next day, the family, now in a wholly altered frame of mind and my own homecoming turning almost into a negligible side event in the larger drama, trudged to the prison to visit my half-brother. Because of martial law now in effect, soldiers guarded everything with their drawn rifles, some with bayonets fixed at the muzzle. I was shocked to see my half-brother so big and heavy, nothing like the athletic man that I had last seen at the Yongsan master's house some years ago. It almost frightened me that the prison guards might have tortured him overnight to such swollen proportions. No, he had just become such a big man in the ensuing years of good life as a civilian. Given the circumstances he faced, my little fate was wholly insignificant and he barely acknowledged in my direction. The three adults discussed the strategy for the upcoming court martial and mentioned that the leader of Faction-A was going to defend him at the trial. The leader said that was the least he could do for the services my half-brother had rendered his cause. All sorts of speculation and hearsay were mentioned and discussed, alternately optimistic and pessimistic. I heard that the leader of Faction-B, their nemesis, was a nasty sort, which rendered their mood pessimistic. On the other hand, the leader of Faction-A was a good lawyer and had a strong sense of loyalty and obligation, which made them optimistic.

While I have little or no memory of how the next few days were spent, I vividly remember the trial. The trial was held at a civilian courthouse now converted to hold military courts martial. As we settled in the courthouse facing the judges, the prisoners, about half a dozen of them, including my half-brother, were brought in from the side door. They all faced the judges, with their backs turned to the audience. The chief judge announced that the court was now in session. At this announcement, the soldiers with carbines and bayonets, lining up on both sides, cocked their rifles in unison. This military's move made a terrifying metallic sound that reverberated throughout the courtroom. Along with this military maneuver, a chill went down my spine— a scary, ill omen. One of the defendants was a civilian, accused of having kicked a man to death while intoxicated. Apparently, he had a dirty foot, shoes caked with dirt, with which he had kicked the victim. The prosecutor, a military man, described it as a 'dirt foot,' using the Chinese word *'to-jok,'* that killed the victim. One of the three judges asked the prosecutor what a 'dirt foot' (*to-jok*) was, and the crowd broke into laughter. The prosecutor explained that it meant a shoe with a lot of dirt on it, with which the defendant had kicked the victim to death. This explanation obviously satisfied the judges and they went on with the next questions. Aside from the dirt-foot questions and answers, I have no recollection of the trial, except for the sentencing. I don't remember the details of how the leader of Faction-A, my half-brother's obligatory lawyer, defended him.

After the trial was over and a quick recess later, the court was reconvened for the sentencing. Once again, the soldiers cocked their rifles, whose metallic sound was not as terrifying as the first time. The three-judge panel returned to their seats and one of them read the sentences for each of the defendants. I only remember the sentences of the homicidal kicker with a 'dirt foot' and that of my half-brother, because both received identical three-year sentences. The lawyer told my stepmother that it was unfair that a murderer and an honorable soldier received the same sentence. There was no appeal from court martial sentences, and my half-brother was destined to serve every minute of those three years.

My other half-brother, the rice-taker, came home more often. But as before when we were younger, he paid little or no sympathetic attention to me. He spent most of the visits with his buddies on the boxing team who traveled with him. On my part, I visited some of my old school classmates, one of them in particular whose father did business between Jeju Island and the mainland. The family had come from Jeju Island themselves, and my friend always teased me that I must have come from Jeju Island because I had that 'typical Jeju face.' I had no knowledge of Jeju Island and laughed off his Jeju reference. (It is true, however, that people used to say that I had the 'island look.') After meeting my friends and spending time with them, I had to come home at night, to a now very gloomy and hopeless household. With the head of their house held in prison for three long years to come and no hope of appeal or clemency possible, the gloom and hopelessness could not feel heavier. Soon, in recognition of these miserable circumstances, the live-in mistress said goodbye to us all and left to live with her mother in her old hometown, likely to resume her former profession of hairdressing. In a sad household, the absence of a vibrant young woman is quite noticeable and her empty spot could not be filled by anybody. I was never good at small talk and the ten-year separation kept us from being like a real family. My free half-brother was jovial and seemed to make my stepmother forget for a few moments that her older son was in prison. But I could not be part of these mother-son interactions. Old memories of my stepmother were returning again as my 'Big Mother' and it was not a good development.

As expected, my situation was rapidly becoming dire. I had come home full of hope and possibilities, but with the flip of fate, everything had disappeared. The cruelty of this transformed fortune was bearable only because it was gradual. Evil had crept on me little by little each day. From his arrest to his prison term, the reality took place over so many days, in which every day added just a little more gloom and doom in my realization of what was happening. Each day, I had adjusted to the new shock. I could hardly notice a letter that my storeowner's brother sent me, asking how I was doing with my family and the new college I was attending, ending the letter by kindly reminding me to send his pants back if I was done with them. My fate now seemed much more desperate than the breach of courtesy by which

I failed to send somebody's pants back. Besides, I still had only one pair of pants and there was no way I could send him this pair, as I was presently wearing them. Each day was becoming more and more difficult and more and more uncomfortable for me as part of the household. On her part, my stepmother said nothing about my future or my present burden on her household. To me, her silence was loud with meaning. After ten years of exile, I was now back in the same place I was ten years ago, an unwelcome stepson who was consuming her food. As an unconscious habit, I sighed all the time while I was sitting on the wooden platform overlooking the garden. In despair and hopelessness, I was becoming like an old man. Often, my stepmother sighed in synchronicity as if to respond to my own despair and hopelessness. She sighed for her son in prison, and I sighed for my hope in tatters. Without him, my hitherto hero-brother, being the bridge over our horrid past, my stepmother and I were once again on a collision course. According to my destiny, and its providence, this collision course meant that something was about to happen. Didn't something always happen when my life was at the end of its rope? But what?

It was one night. Darkness had fallen over the garden and we were once again sitting on the wooden platform, sighing uncomfortably and uncontrollably, but in unconscious synchronicity. We had stopped drinking tea long ago, and recently my stepmother and I started sharing our sighs. Then my stepmother said something that left me thunderstruck.

"You know, your mother was looking for you," she said. But she said it so matter-of-factly that she could have said it was raining outside.

I repeated the phrase to myself. "Your mother was looking for you." My mother was looking for me? The last time my mother was mentioned was my stepmother's criticism of her for making breakfast without first washing her hands. Now this stepmother of mine was telling me that my mother was looking for me? The significance of the past tense, as she said my mother "was" looking for me, stuck in my mind, and that sounded ominous. Trembling with fear and hope, I was thinking immediately that she *was* looking for me and now she was *no longer* looking for me?

"Where is she?" Dumbstruck, I asked about a person who I didn't know existed. My whole life's future hung in the balance on the answer to this question.

"She lives in Tokyo," my stepmother said, and to my great relief, in the present tense. So my real mother was alive and lived in Tokyo, and was looking for me.

"Looking for me, how?" My stepmother said my mother sent one of my first-cousins and her nephew, named Akira, whom she had raised in Tokyo for her older sister. Akira made regular visits to Korea, his homeland, where he had connections with family and friends, and my mother asked him to find me.

My heart was now pounding in anticipation. My mother was still alive and lived in Tokyo! Wait a minute. *Why did she wait so long to look for me?*

Tokyo was good news and bad news. Good news meant that she was probably rich as everybody in Japan was rich (certainly relative to poor Korea). And it was bad news because she lived in another country which, thanks to Syngman Rhee's rigid anti-Japan policy, had no formal relations with Korea. Only letters were allowed. Traveling between Japan and Korea was highly restricted and phone calls were impossible. Tokyo was only two hours away by plane, but might as well have been at the North Pole.

"Why didn't you tell him where I was?" I asked, incredulous. I was still recovering from the shock. She said she didn't know where I was at the time my cousin from Tokyo called on her. (Not true, because my half-brother had visited me in Seoul where I was a houseboy, and I could always be traced through there.)

"So, what did you tell my cousin who was looking for me?"

"I told him that you were dead," she said very calmly, considering the content of what she was saying and the storm it was creating in me.

"How could you have said that," I raised my voice, disbelieving, "when you knew where I was, and I was not dead?!"

"We didn't know where you were, and you did not write to us all this time," she said regretfully, as if she were sorry she had missed my birthday. It was true I had not written them, but that was just a technicality. I could have always been traced through the Yongsan house in Seoul. They could have also located me through newspaper and radio advertisements. Such things were common in post-war Korea where so many families had been separated. So the Wicked Witch of the West, waving her evil magic wand, had told my Cousin Akira that I was dead! I was not dead. I was very much alive, just struggling to find three meals a

173

day! How I could have avoided all that suffering if this woman had told Akira the truth, or had made some effort to find me!

Then she dropped another one: "Your cousin came back this year looking for you again!" she said, slowly tightening her torture machine, and added that she had told the searching cousin the same thing: little Sei-Kan was dead. Why would my stepmother say such a mean lie? For many years thereafter, this question to which there seemed to be no answer bothered me. *Why did my stepmother tell my cousin that I was dead?* To hide her guilt of mistreating me? Very likely. To still keep me in her family because I was such a treasure of genius, just in case I turned into something spectacular? Very flattering but not likely. Because she *really* believed that I was dead? Somewhat likely, but that fact could have been verified easily in a tiny country like Korea. I was merely searching for ways in which my stepmother could have found me. On the other hand, from her point of view, there was every reason to simply, and easily, tell the search party that since I had not written to her, I was dead; no news from a person for close to ten years in post-war Korea was most likely indicative of his demise. Indeed, no news and death were commonly connected in most people's minds. But I was in no mood to be generous with analysis and understanding. I was in shock and, understandably, in fury! Things were so shocking, exulting, infuriating, and disappointing that my head was spinning with no coherent thoughts in it.

So, let's calm down and think, I told myself. *First, back to the present bombshell. My mother is alive and lives in Tokyo. Most urgently, how do I find out where she lives?*

"How do I find out where she lives?" I asked.

My stepmother sighed sadly. "Maybe the Spring Garden Portrait Studio would know?" She said the old man at the studio, my mother's good friend, had also moved to Japan a few years ago and his son continued the portrait business. Maybe he was still in business at the old studio and still in contact with his father in Tokyo who would know my mother's address in the same city.

Instantly, I sprang into action and was on my way to the 'Spring Garden' portrait studio. If I had wings, I would have flown at super speed. In the past, I had walked by the studio many times on my way to elementary school and to Sunday school, which was located at the church next to the two-story red brick building which had my father's print-shop and the studio. The portrait studio and the red brick building were reminders of my happier times. Now the studio and the red brick building, completely forgotten since then, were suddenly thrust into my life again as the slender thread that tied me to my mother. It was somewhat late at night and the studio, if it was still in business, could be closed. But there was no way I could wait until the next day. It was tonight, right now, or I would die. My heart was pounding with excitement and fury, excitement at the news that my mother was alive and looking for me, fury at the fact that my stepmother hid me from my mother's people! I had never received such a shock as that night and my head was throbbing and my heart was pounding like mad.

The most significant emotional reaction at the moment was that I was no longer an orphan. I wanted to shout to the world! Being without parents had been like being born without arms or legs. I had to answer the unasked question from everyone: why are you without them? I now had a family, a family on my mother's side who loved me enough to look for me! All the loneliness, all the poverty, all the sadness, all the misery, all the pain, all the darkness and hopelessness that I had suffered my whole life, almost ten years of solitary survival, all such emotional replays were racing in my head. This emotion alone overrode all other emotional reactions and I was just relieved and happy with the news. Like many of my friends, I had a mother and family! I was no longer an orphan, alone in the world and on the street!

The studio was only a few blocks away, but it seemed like miles. I finally reached the building and, thank God, it was still a portrait business. And it was still open! I pushed open the studio door and a man in his forties looked at me somewhat strangely. Obviously, I didn't look like a person who was ready for a studio portrait, more like a distraught youth on the run or a plain madman. I told him who I was, and it was now his turn to be a distraught madman, as he was looking at a boy who had died a long time ago.

"What? I thought you were dead!" the studio man said, disbelieving his own eyes. "Your Cousin Akira told me. He stopped by last year and this year and said that's what your stepmother told him!"

Akira had told the studio man about the hard task of telling my mother in Tokyo the heartbreaking news of the bubbly boy, Sei-Kan, who was dead. Isn't there a myth somewhere that if you are mistakenly declared dead, you are likely to live very long? I had died twice!

The first breathless question I asked the studio man was perhaps the most important question of my life. "Would your father, who is in Tokyo, know my mother's address in the same city?"

The studio man said no. His father, a good friend of my mother, had moved to Tokyo two years ago, but died recently. There was no way to trace my mother's current address or her name (as most Koreans in Japan had adopted a Japanese name). He told me one fact that answered my burning question as to why my mother had waited this long to send Akira to Korea to look for me. Two years previously when the old studio man moved to Tokyo, he told my mother the news that my father had died toward the end of the war. She was quite surprised to hear of my father's early death, at forty-four, for he had always been known as a man of robust health. So, my mother did not know that my father had died until two years ago. She instantly recognized that my life under the stepmother would be a miserable one without my father. (Akira told the studio man that my mother's first reaction when she heard that my father had died was, "My poor baby Sei-Kan!") Then, she immediately sent Akira to search for me as soon as she had heard of my father's death. The studio man said, when Akira told my mother that her son was dead, she didn't believe it and sent Akira again this spring. I didn't understand whether my mother disbelieving my death meant she didn't trust the stepmother or she was simply denying the possibility that her son had actually died.

Although my mother's whereabouts were still unknown, the studio man told me a few facts that were important and I had not known before. Yes, as my Jeju friend had insisted, my mother's family was from Jeju Island and her family still lived there. The studio man

177

recalled evil days and said my mother wept all the time after losing me in the war of custody to my father. It was such a sad sight that strangers were prompted to ask, "Why would such a pretty woman weep all the time?" Yes, brokenhearted and in utter sorrow after her family had failed to take me back from my father, she wept her way to Japan, leaving her own trail of tears, the studio man said. Fortunately for me, the studio man was quite up to date on all these things because Akira had used the studio man as the contact point. This year and the year before, he came by the studio and updated the studio man with useful information. One of the most important pieces of information he gave me was that Akira's younger brother, a medical doctor, had just finished his internship and left Gwangju. The studio man did not keep my mother's address in Tokyo because it was pointless. After all, her son was dead. Nor did he keep the address of my doctor-cousin, Akira's younger brother. As far as the studio man was concerned, he said, the case concerning me was closed. I was dead and everybody else also closed the book on me. However, my mother, on the irrational and stubborn hope against hope, had refused to close the book on me. Refusing to believe the news of my death, because she believed that my stepmother had lied or was mistaken about her information, my mother sent Akira to Korea to look for me again. But she was told again that I had died. *Did she believe it when told the same news for the second time?* I wondered. The bad blood between the two scorned women was still bad and still thick years later. (Rest their souls! Both unhappy women are dead now.) The most precious information for me was that my mother's family still lived on Jeju Island, which was now becoming a popular honeymoon spot in Korea; my doctor-cousin was a recent graduate of the medical school in Gwangju, which could be traced, but there were neither names, nor addresses nor photographs of anyone connected to me, at least for now. It was still all a dead end.

Recovering our wits and senses, the studio man and I discussed what to do. All the shocking news was now out of the way and some practical hard work was ahead. We had to piece together what was in essence a shattered trail. I could go to the medical school the next day and ask the dean if I could look at all the photographs of those recently enrolled medical students who were from Jeju Island. After all, it's a small island, and how many students from the island could there be enrolled at the medical school? I never knew what my cousin looked like, and finding him from the pictures was the classic Korean allusion to an impossible task, which was 'shooting at the stars and hitting one.' I had to find him and this was one of the closest connections open to us. In the meantime, the studio man said he had a box of old photographs kept from his father's days. Could we be lucky enough to find some old photos of my mother and me as a baby still in the box? He searched through some old boxes and found one box that had old black-and-white photos, some of which had faded to yellow. He and I waded through the stacks and were delighted to find several photos of my mother and me as a baby. That was the first image of my mother that I had ever seen in my life. She was beautiful but frail and sad-looking, mostly in traditional Korean garments, holding a chubby baby wearing fashionable western-style clothes. I held in my hand the pictures of my mother, a stranger who was my mother that I never thought existed. We chose one in particular that had me and my mother together in front of a well-recognized waterfall on the island. Now we had something tangible to help our search. We decided that I would write a letter to the newspaper on Jeju Island and enclose the photo of my mother and me and ask the paper to run the photo with a brief story. Then I would visit the medical school and see if I could find anyone who looked like me, surely like looking to hit a star in the sky, and go from there. The kind studio man said he would make a copy of my baby photo to send it to the island newspaper.

It was close to midnight when the studio man and I ended our discussions and reminiscences. We still had nothing concrete and we had no idea yet how to locate my mother or my mother's people. But the fact that I had a family who was looking for me was such a shocking turn of fortunes that I was still quite beside myself. I had never had a moment in my life like then, when I left the studio, with such mixed emotions—anger and happiness, hope and desperation, jubilance and frustration, all mixed and taking turns occupying my head, my heart and my spirit. I had come home full of hope only to witness my savior, my hero-brother, being imprisoned for three long years. Then just as I had reached the depth of despair, I heard the news that my mother, alive and somewhere in Tokyo, was looking for me. The old studio man who knew my mother's address in Tokyo had died. My two cousins, Akira and the doctor, who were looking for me, were at large, their names (Akira was a common first name in Japan.), faces, and addresses unknown. My mother, who I thought had never existed, not only existed but was looking for me. For my stepmother's family, I was either a *persona non grata* or a scourge of God; from my own mother's side, I was the object of her love she desperately wanted to locate. I was barely nineteen, at the end of my teen years, but my emotional state could not have been so extremely broken up into opposites. I was wearing somebody's borrowed pants. Yet, my mother somewhere in Tokyo could have bought me a dozen pairs of pants instantly. My happiness was just around the corner. Yet, it might as well be permanently out of reach. I was in the most miserable spot with my stepmother. Yet, I could escape it in one moment if I could just find where my people were. One family of mine wanted me dead; the other family wanted to find me.

Once I was out into the coolness of the night, on the way home, I was suddenly struck by the evil that my stepmother had done and I hated her all over again. I had to go home to face her again and the enormous reality of how to deal with my treacherous stepmother and my agitated state of emotion loomed large. It was my stepmother who had opened this new door of hope and happiness. After all, she told me about my mother and her people looking for me. But it was my stepmother also who had blocked the slender path that could have led to my happiness. I became angry that my agony had all been caused by her. All of my previous hatefulness toward her came alive again, this time multiplied. The callousness and cruelty of this woman who had denied me the normal comfort of childhood did it a second time. She heartlessly destroyed a boy's life twice. My hate for her was so great that the more I thought about her meanness, the more my hate grew. But I still had to go home and sleep there every night under the same roof and eat her food at the same table. All the while, I would be searching for my mother, following up the thread that was thin and frail, all because of my wicked stepmother. My wicked stepmother who had caused all this for me was asleep when I returned home late that night, and I had a very fitful night's sleep. In my anger and fury at her, of course, I had not thought about raising the question: What if my stepmother had kept it all secret about my mother or Akira's visits, and took it to her grave? Of course, in all likelihood, I would have never known about my mother's family even if I had died of starvation or loneliness. The strange woman, who was my stepmother, had killed me with one hand when I was twelve, but was reviving me with the other hand when I was nineteen. Why would she do that? Was she having a battle of conscience within herself, the two sides in her, good and evil, debating which side was going to win? The vagaries of the human heart, and I would never know the answer.

Next day, my search started at the Spring Garden Studio, which had become the headquarters for our search mission. First, we wrote a letter to the island newspaper complete with the photo of my mother, holding me in her arms, posing in front of a waterfall quite popular on the island as a tourist spot. Then, I made my trek to the medical school. The dean, whom my query at the school had led to, was a very nice man who agreed to help me with my quest. He would select all the applications of former and present students from Jeju Island for me to examine. The applications had photos of the applicants so I could do the 'best-resemblance' test. My assumption that there would be hardly more than a dozen candidates from the island was wrong. There were over fifty applications, all with photos, and finding somebody who looked like me from the photos was worse than the proverbial shooting at the stars. All the faces in the photos looked bright and earnest, and I would whisper to each of them, "Are you my cousin?" After hours of guessing and re-guessing, I selected the best dozen and took down their boarding house addresses in the city and their home addresses on the island. But it was in the middle of the summer vacation and, when I actually looked into their boarding houses, I found that all of the residents had gone home for the summer. I succeeded in locating about half a dozen boarding houses that day. But only three owners of the boarding houses were actually on the premises. When they heard my story, these owners were very kind and allowed me to search the rooms to see if there was anything, a letter or picture or something, that indicated he was my cousin that I was looking for. When my search turned up nothing, they were very sympathetic and I was very disheartened.

It was both emotionally and physically exhausting. Emotionally, the stakes were high, as my life depended on finding my cousin. Physically, I was on foot, walking all over the city, trying to locate one boarding house after another. It was midsummer—hot, humid, and depressing. The demoralizing search, not knowing exactly what I was searching for, with no name and no face, had me discouraged further and further each day. My search only led to another dead end. One of the medical students, present and past, was my doctor-cousin, Akira's younger brother, both sons of my mother's older sister who had joined forces with my mother years ago in the battle over me, against my father and his men. Fifteen years later, that little boy was now searching desperately for his family, every step seemingly ending in vain. Of the half dozen finalists whose boarding houses I eventually searched, there were three that I considered hopeful, just relying on my instinctive hunch and reaction to the faces in the photos. I wrote them a letter each, explaining whom I was searching for, and ended up asking each recipient to write me back if he was indeed my first cousin. I was desperate, caught between hope and despair, and I did not want to go back to the street or three-meals-a-day minimal life.

The summer days were moving slowly, and my days of searching and waiting continued to turn up nothing. There was no response from the Jeju Island newspaper. All three persons whom I had written individual letters to replied to me very kindly and sympathetically. But all of them said, "No, I am not your cousin." They all promised to keep their eyes open in case they heard anything to that effect. After all, they suggested that the island cohort stuck together and met each other often. So, not to despair too much, anything was possible. Every day, I stopped by the studio to report what I had done, and to inquire if there was any news (as I used the studio's address for my letters). Every day, it was always, "Sorry, nothing today."

In the meantime, my situation at home with my stepmother, who was becoming increasingly more like the Big Mother, was deteriorating alarmingly. As I became more desperate and despondent with my search and angrier that all my suffering was due to my stepmother, I became more furious with her every day. My fury with her now was actually matching *her own hell's fury* with my father and myself. It was all her evil scheme from her meanness, I told her every time we had a fight, which was virtually every day. We were back to our old hostility, except that now I had my own anger and fury that matched hers. As our fights became more and more frequent, and as our fights became more and more confrontational, I sensed that my days at home with my stepmother were now numbered. I could not continue to be hostile to her while sleeping under her roof and eating her food. Hope was not getting hopeful but despair was getting more despairing daily. The next question was always: *Where would I go?* I had come home with great optimism, but now I had to leave home again, staring into the dark misery of hopelessness and loneliness. Hot and wilting, the summer was slowly passing by and I was trudging here and there, tired and dispirited, searching everywhere for a thread of possibility.

It was exhausting in another way. I had been so *close* to a chance to live a normal life. I had survived the ten years of street life and the harsh existence of a child laborer. Escaping from this precarious life and existence was my desperate prayer every day. The cruelty of almost grasping it when my hero-brother wanted to send me to college, only to be sent to prison himself and crashing my hope to pieces, left me exhausted. Then the cruelty of being told that my mother's family was looking for me to offer me the normal life that I so desperately wanted and, not being able to find them, had pushed me almost to the brink of utter breakdown. I endured the hard life of a laborer as a teenager, with good discipline and strength of character. But this yo-yo swing between heaven and hell, so close to one, yet so far away, so full of hope one minute and so full of despair the next, was almost impossible to endure because of its cruelty to my spirit. For some reason, providence was pushing me to the ultimate limits of endurance.

After one particularly nasty argument with my stepmother, I came to the conclusion that I had to leave home again. There was no way I could look at her face and not get angry at what she had done, denying me that desperate chance at happiness, telling the angel of rescue that I was dead. As my father kept me away from my mother, to start all this chain of misery, now my father's wife kept me away from my mother again, fifteen years later. The goddess of vengeance was on her side. She could declare victory. She had done it. The next day, I packed what little there was as my belongings and told no one in particular that I was leaving. It was the last time I ever saw my stepmother.

I was going back to Seoul. Even unto now, I remember it as the saddest moment of my life. Throughout my short life, it was as if every time I was leaving one place to go to another, it was such a sad desperation that always accompanied me. I was going to stop by the studio to give the man my address in Seoul, my last place of employment, just in case any news came. It was dark and I had to get going to catch the night train. The last time I was on the night train to Seoul, I was ten years younger and ten times the unknowns. Now, the night train was going to be ten times more miserable to face, for I knew that after such high hopes for which I had come home, there was nothing but darkness and misery waiting for me. But I had to stop by the studio and give my address in Seoul, the slender thread and connection to the ever-diminishing hope of finding my family.

The studio man welcomed me into the office when I entered the studio perhaps for the last time. A man in his mid-thirties, in a nice suit, was sitting at the business desk in the office, looking at me curiously. Apparently, the two had been talking with each other. I stood just inside the door, looking at the two men alternately.

"I want you to meet somebody," the studio man said, pointing to the gentleman at the business desk. "Dr. Huer, your brother." (In Korea, cousins are generally referred to as 'brother.')

My doctor-cousin, the man I was searching for all summer, the slender thread that tied me to my mother, was sitting there. As I sat on the chair indicated, he looked at me with deep melancholia and his face was also full of questions. I was so overcome by the relief that I broke down and cried. Once again, fate had snatched me from the threshold of unending misery and darkness. The executioner of life, just as the noose was around my neck and the lever was about to be pulled, declared that I was reprieved, and that I would live, not die. My brother, the doctor, waited for me to collect myself and asked gently what I had been doing all my life. The last time he had seen me, I was a bubbly baby of three and he was a teenager. I told him, between sobs, that I had worked at different factories and as a houseboy, and that I left the last factory in Inchon because it had closed. I told him that I had come home to Gwangju to go to college but my half-brother had gone to prison on a three-year sentence. And I had nowhere to go, so I was getting ready to go back to Seoul and see what I could do there.

"What kind of friends do you keep?" he asked. I told him I had not many friends but most were now in college. He asked if I drank or smoked (a sort of quick way of judging one's moral standing). I said, "No, I never did." He asked about my education, and I told him I never went beyond the sixth grade, but passed the college entrance exam. My brother, the doctor, asked me some more questions to make sure he was not looking at a vagabond street urchin who had turned bad. He seemed to be satisfied that, after all that, I had grown up a fairly decent lad.

Then the studio man joined us and turned to the discussion of fate that had brought us together on the strength of the thinnest thread and chance. The doctor had come to Gwangju on a government assignment in lieu of full military service, and was on the way back home when he ran into an old medical school friend, several years his junior, on the bus.

"Weren't you looking for a first cousin?" the friend asked. Somehow, he might have heard that rumor.

"Yes, we were looking for our first cousin, the son of my aunt who lives in Japan. But he is dead," said my cousin. "My older brother, Akira, came to Korea last year from Japan and earlier this year again to look for him. But his family told my brother that he had died, and so he reported that to my aunt in Tokyo."

"I got a letter from him," his junior friend said. "Obviously, the poor fellow thought I was you."

His friend told him how I had obtained his address from the medical school and, thinking he might be my brother, I had written him a letter. Then, miraculously, they had run into each other on the bus! My cousin, the doctor, was shocked that Sei-kan had come back from the dead! He bolted up from his seat and hollered, "My God, I need to stop at the studio." Just at that exact moment, the bus was passing by the portrait studio.

"Stop, driver!" my cousin hollered. "Stop the bus!" The startled bus driver brought the bus to a screeching halt and let my cousin off. He walked straight to the studio where he and Akira had congregated a few times before while they had been looking for me. The studio man told my cousin all that he knew about me—how I had come home because my boxer-brother promised to send me to college, how my boxer-brother was sent to prison, how my stepmother had told Akira that I was dead, how I went to the medical school and looked at the photos to find my cousin the doctor, (In fact, he was not one of the dozen that I had selected from the medical school files as 'best candidates.') how we wrote the newspaper a letter and were waiting for its response, and how desperately I was looking for my mother and her family because I had nobody else to turn to.

While the two had been talking to each other, I walked in to say goodbye to the studio man before I got on the night train to nowhere. But as it happened so many times, I was saved by the hook of the angels just in the nick of time, who pulled me up to heaven, like Faust, from the jaws of hell. In the invisible network of chance and design, so many people, here and there and everywhere, like the studio man, the medical school friend of my brother's, maybe even my deceased father, extended their hands and helped me cross that one extra step. So, instead of falling into the abyss and oblivion, I would land in the safety of the solid ground to take the next steps with my life.

That night, my brother, the doctor, took me to his house and introduced me to his family, his wife, and two young boys. They looked at me shyly and whispered among themselves about this poor relation, who had been dropped into their midst. But they were sweet and welcoming. The doctor's wife, my sister-in-law, a very kind and generous-looking woman in her early thirties, was exceedingly comforting. That night, I slept for the first time in nearly ten years with peace and hope in my heart and among the people that were my family. I was saved by my true mother and her people. Irony of all ironies, it was my evil stepmother who made the ultimate link between me and my family. It was my evil stepmother who had pushed this young boy into the stormy sea, and it was also my evil stepmother who threw me the lifesaver just as I was drowning.

The next day, my doctor-brother sent me to Jeju Island to meet my relatives, especially the two aunts: the older aunt who was my mother's older sister and the mother of my two first cousins, Akira who came from Tokyo to search for me and the doctor who found me. The other aunt, my mother's younger sister, who lived near the main port on the island, was my first visit. The passenger ship I took to get to the island had set sail in the late evening and docked early the following morning, and when I knocked on my younger aunt's door, the family with several girls was at the breakfast table. I was properly introduced and, after some fuss of welcome, joined their breakfast table. One more small drama had to play out while we were in the middle of our eating. An older lady flung the gate open, hollering loudly, "Look, look, look! What's in the paper! It's Sei-Kan!" She was waving a copy of the Island's morning newspaper that had a story of me and my mother, with a picture that the studio man had sent to the newspaper that seemed like an eternity ago.

"Well, look what we have *here*!" my younger aunt said, calmly pointing to me. (The old lady was my mother and my younger aunt's cousin.) After a good laugh, the older aunt joined us and many stories were repeated.

I was soon sent to the other side of the island where, in the second largest city, Soguipo, my older aunt, my mother's older sister, lived. Her husband, who had been the former mayor of the city, was still called 'Mr. Mayor' by the town's people. My aunt's family owned a small hotel on a hilltop overlooking the ocean and I stayed in one of the rooms at the hotel for the next few months, enjoying the beauty of the island and the warmth of my mother's family. One of the first things that my mother's family did was to remove me from the stepmother's family records and enter me into the mayor's family register so that I officially became Akira's and the doctor's youngest brother. The doctor, now my legitimate brother, told the presiding judge that his father, the mayor, had sired me in his wild-oats days and only recently found me on the mainland. The judge agreed with the explanation as to how I came to be entering his family register at nineteen. From this point on, we became 'brothers,' both in spirit and in law.

VI. Return to Laughter

When the initial excitement died down, a clan council was held on the island to determine what to do with this new member of the family. All agreed that my career would be best served if I became a doctor. I would prepare for the national exam to qualify for an admission to a medical school, very likely my brother's alma mater in Gwangju. This decision gambled on the potential of my intellectual talent, which was by then considered quite superior. I ordered the books specially designed for the thousands of home-schoolers like me who had missed their chance to attend regular schools and began to take my study seriously. Then a letter came from my doctor-brother in which he invited me to come and stay with him while I was preparing for this all-important exam. The letter said I could also help him with the government health center that he was running in a remote rural village. I was happy for this change of the scenery, since the paradise island had begun to lose its novelty somewhat by then. I packed my books and, for once in my life, moved to a new location with an anticipation of happiness and peace of mind. In fact, the one year that I spent with my brother's family, studying to be a doctor and helping him at his government clinic in this remote village, was one of the happiest periods of my life.

The government healthcare center that my brother was running, half of which was used as our family quarters, was located in a small farming village, about a hundred miles southwest of Gwangju. (I do not recall its name. Korea's administrative structure divides the nation into eight states, called 'Do,' in which the largest units are the cities, like Seoul or Gwangju. The areas outside the cities are divided into counties, called 'Gun,' which is further divided into towns, called 'Eup,' which is further divided into the smallest villages, called 'Myun.' My brother was assigned to this Village Myun because he had served in the military for less than six months, as he received a medical discharge only after five months. Hence, he had to serve minimum three years as a government doctor in remote places.) It was so small and remote that it had only one bus a day coming and going on its dirt road that connected it to the nearest county seat a few miles away. The main dirt road tapered off as it wound by the mountains on both sides of the road and ended with the last of the remotest mountains. Villagers and farmers with their small farms lived scattered along both sides of the road. They converged on market days, which came about every five days, at the town square near the village government office, to ride the bus to the county-seat. Our government health clinic was on the other side of the village office across the street, facing the crowd on market days. Around the village office was a cluster of mom-and-pop stores that sold candies for kids and cigarettes and alcohol for adults. The village head, the richest man there, whose son was away in college studying to be a lawyer, lived in a very large wooden house about a block away from his office. As the two authoritative leaders of the village, one civil and one medical, the village head and my brother became good friends and we attended many of the other family functions.

It was a typical rural village with no medical facility, to which the new military rulers chose to send their government doctors to offer modern medicine. Fraught with superstition and ignorance, but with the heart of gold, the villagers largely stuck to their traditional means of healthcare. As such they often preferred shamanism and obtained their medicines from one small drugstore whose pharmacist had functioned as their *de facto* doctor. Naturally, the pharmacist welcomed my brother, the modern medicine doctor, on the surface, but we knew my brother's modern medicine was going to hurt his business. Whenever I could, I accompanied my brother on his house calls. Unless we lucked out with an official vehicle, which happened on rare occasions, we mostly walked on our house calls. Although the services rendered by the government healthcare center were free, the villagers often brought stuff from their farms, such as chickens, potatoes, and vegetables, to show their gratitude. Since my sister-in-law loathed killing, it was my job to prepare the chicken, by twisting the neck until it was dead, and pluck the feathers expertly with boiling water, using my experience learned in Rock Hill.

I helped my brother also as the clinic's record-keeper when, aside from the specialized medical records, the paperwork was largely routine. Most of these routine records were kept in English. One day, a fairly intoxicated man stopped by the center looking for a prescription for his ulcer. Since my brother was away at the time, I looked through old records and found an 'ulcer prescription,' which happened to have been in English. I copied the prescription and handed it to the ulcerous man. He looked at the prescription written in total gibberish and got very upset.

"With all due respect, sir," the intoxicated man with an ulcer said, holding up the prescription written mostly in English, "I know you spent many years to learn all this, but do you have to write the prescription in German that I cannot read?"

I apologized for his inconvenience but assured him that the pharmacist in the county seat would be able to read what was written on it. He finally left but was not wholly satisfied with my explanation. Otherwise, the villagers were largely respectful toward the new government doctor and his family, even though English was quite alien to them. Unbeknownst to me, the rumors of my English knowledge had spread to the people who worked at the village office and the teachers at the elementary school in the village. Often, they sought out my help with their English issues. That summer, the village head started the town's only refrigeration services for the farmers' slaughtered animals on the way to the market. He wanted to have a nice-sounding English advertisement on his new service and consulted me. After some consideration, I recommended, "Keeping cool, keeping fresh," which immensely satisfied the village head who made the sayings his company logo. My fame had apparently spread to other villages as well. A social worker in the neighboring village asked me if I could give her English lessons once a week, which I agreed to do. The social worker, a lady in her late thirties, lived alone in her one-room boarding house and made me dinner in exchange for her English lessons. It turned out she made me more than my dinner, and, as a healthy young man going on twenty, I accepted her weekly female largesse gladly.

Korea was going through what the economists later called an economic 'takeoff,' a significant turning point at which a country moves from underdevelopment to development in a very noticeable way. Park Chung Hee, the head of the military junta that had taken over Korea, was largely responsible for this remarkable economic leap in a country that had perennially been poor. On the strength of his material accomplishment, he left the military and was running for president as a civilian and as the man who was pushing Korea into the modern world. On Election Day, my brother and I went to the elementary school, our voting place, and cast our votes, I for Park and my brother very likely for Park also. That was my first voting ever. Other than that, our village was peaceful and, other than the new refrigeration service, there was no sign of economic development or industrial progress in our village.

Well, there *was* a small event that was revolutionary enough to shake up the very traditional-minded rural village. The son of the village head who was away in college studying to become a lawyer (which would also qualify to be a judge and a prosecutor) passed the law exam and was appointed a judge, and he was only twenty-five years old! There was a huge feast at the village head's large house to celebrate this monumental accomplishment for a country boy! But the country boy who made good in a big way shocked everybody by asking them to call him 'Your Honor' (in Korean *'yong-gam-nim'*). The honorific title not only referred to the official judgeship but also was in recognition of being a person of high seniority that generally comes with advanced age. It was scandalous that a twenty-five-year-old new judge was telling everybody he wanted to be called 'Your Honor.'

"Imagine that," my brother was furious as we were walking home from the feast. "He wants to be called 'Your Honor,' and he is only twenty-five!"

Aside from this scandal, which the village forgot about quickly, as the new judge was soon assigned to a very faraway place, peace returned to the village. I thoroughly enjoyed living with my brother's family, and my nephews, all under ten years old, who were fully cooperative with my belated childhood. We concocted all sorts of playful acts to entertain their parents and ourselves. One of the popular acts was what we called the 'Ben-Hur Chariot Race,' whereby the oldest two boys would be the horses and the third boy would be Ben-Hur who rode on the backs of the two oldest boys who ran around the house on their knees. Under my prankster's direction, the boys also cooperated with the mischief of purloining persimmons and pomegranates, even before their season, from our neighbors, all to my sister-in-law's continuous objections. (Maybe my old habits die hard!) The darkness that had always hovered over my life was finally lifted, and my memories of the teen years seemed to have vanished. If anyone from the Rock Hill factory days, where I was the designated human engine and clay smasher, saw me here, he would not have recognized me. I was happy and my future was cloudless. In this nameless village, my soul received its healing strength and my mind was freed from its perennial sorrowfulness. The village people only knew me as the brother of their government doctor who was preparing to become a doctor himself. My dignity and pride, so long under attack from cruel reality, were now mine again. I became a full human being in this nameless humble farming village!

It was about this time, when I perhaps had recovered myself from my earlier years that I received a draft notice from the military, which obligated all Korean young men to serve. In the summer of the following year, in 1962, I reported to the military. But my military draft turned out to be another pivotal point because it gave me a highly coveted chance to serve in the U.S. Army, thanks to my considerable English talent, as a 'Korean Augmentation.' A Korean augmentation in essence was a soldier on loan from the Korean government to the American military to make up for the latter's manpower shortage. This not only opened the door for me to go to America where I got married and started a family, but it also opened me to American society itself, for I spent most of the three years in the U.S. military studying America's history, culture and people, and most seriously of all, its destiny as the world's only nation created to advance individual freedom.

VII. Postscript

Now, my narrative returns to the two mothers, my stepmother and my real mother. I met my real mother at Narita Airport in Tokyo, Japan, in 1965, twenty-two years after she had left the little boy in Gwangju. By then, we had exchanged photographs and letters, and even talked on the phone many times on the military communication systems of which I took advantage. But it was overshadowed by the uncertainty of feelings that I was meeting my real mother for the first time in my living memory. On her part, the emotional impact of her first meeting with her son, whom she had left when he was three, was quite beyond my imagination. Even though I had given her my flight schedule, she did not quite believe that her son was really coming to see her in Tokyo. After all, she had been told twice that her son was dead, and this very son was coming to see her in the flesh. On the train ride from Tokyo to Narita Airport, her prayerful heart received a largely positive omen when a passenger, sitting next to her on the train and carrying a huge bouquet of flowers, left the bundle on his seat when he got off the train. Shocked by this unexpected 'gift' from a stranger, she considered that a good omen. Her son *was* really coming. She thanked providence which had brought her the flowers, a gift from a stranger who had merely sat next to her. As I walked into the airport lounge, my mother and I immediately recognized each other. She looked exactly the way she did in the photographs I had seen. We hugged and she gave me the flowers and told me the story behind the gift from a stranger. We had tea at the airport's coffee shop, uncertainly looking at each other as mother and son, for all practical purposes, for the first time. There was much distance between us, both factual and emotional, that we had to overcome and fill. Mother asked how my stepmother had been doing. I said that, aside from hearing about her stroke that paralyzed her left arm, I had heard little about my former stepmother for many years. My mother looked very sad and lowered her face when my stepmother was mentioned. I understood how my mother was feeling about my former stepmother who had so mistreated her son, even pronouncing him dead. Yet, my mother herself had been very much part of the woman's misery. When Mother asked how I had survived my childhood, I told her that providence had protected me at the worst moments of my life. Each time I felt I had come to the end of my rope, I said, a benevolent hand stretched out and scooped me up from the abyss of trouble. Then she said something that I have never forgotten; she said it so casually, as if it was so true that no emphasis was needed, "Your father must be taking care of you from heaven."

My father, giving me the helping hand whenever I needed it the most, all through the days of hunger and the nights of loneliness? Why had I not ever thought of that before? If my life had been favored by providence, why couldn't it be my father who had been the central thrust of that providential force? All my life, especially in my young years, I had been so absorbed in my own struggle, so aware of my own suffering, that I had so seldom thought that there were other people around me, like my mother and my father, who were praying for me and were interceding with the benevolent force in my behalf. This casual comment by my mother suddenly humbled me and I was once again reminded of the fathomless depth and unlimited possibilities that providence rendered our lives on Earth. Wasn't it my hated stepmother who, in her merciful moment, also connected me to my mother and her family that scooped me up off the street?

Almost ten years after I had met my mother, I went back to Korea. I took my son Jonathan, then three, to see my former stepmother in Gwangju. I had forgiven her completely by then and had no more of those nightmares that she had caused me for years. I did not meet her because, according to her daughter-in-law that I talked to, she was out somewhere with her senior citizens' group. Her daughter-in-law, the wife of my half-brother who used to steal my food and posted me as a guard at the nocturnal outhouse, was herself widowed, as my half-brother had died the previous year. (My oldest half-brother who had served every last day of his three-year prison sentence had died not too long after the end of the prison term.) So, my former stepmother had buried three of her four children in her unhappy life. I told the young widow that I used to be part of that family and, introducing Jonathan, I brought my son to meet my former stepmother. The young widow seemed to understand my unspoken word—forgiveness—in whose spirit I had wanted my old stepmother to meet her new grandson. Maybe the word was better left unspoken and maybe it was better that our visit did not materialize. Indeed, what could we have said to each other after we said hello? I did not doubt that when my former stepmother heard that I had brought my son to see her, she would have understood clearly why father and son had come to see her. I heard not too long after the aborted visit that she had died, ending a life that had rarely experienced the loving hand of her legally married husband. My own mother, being much younger than my stepmother, died fifteen years later, in 2003. Both women are now dead and buried, along with their sorrowful lamentations. I am very certain, if what we know about heaven is correct, that they have become good neighbors where none of our Earthly trials and tribulations matters.

Years later, I heard from my good friend, whose parents owned the inn in Gwangju, that my stepmother and my half-brothers, including the older one who had eventually served every day of his three-year sentence, were quite surprised that I had been taken out of their family records. We were now strangers in law as we had been in spirit. When the judge finally ruled that I was now one of the Huers, a member of my mother's family, I had a strange tug of the heart that was a combination of feeling relief and feeling empty at the same time. My stepmother's expulsion of me from her family was the demon that I had fought all my teen life to exorcise. She was the cause of my nightmares for many years, and she was also the embodiment of an evil 'stepmother' that shadowed my entire life. Now, I was out of her family register and we had become proper strangers. My half-brothers were now unrelated to me even in half measures. We were not even 'half' brothers. The half-thick blood between us was now completely diluted to zero. Why did I feel empty when the umbilical cord between my nemesis and me was finally cut, and the lifelong curse was exorcized forever out of my life?

For the rest of my life, I struggled with the questions of how the most important teenage years of my life affected me, my character, and my personality. What happens when a boy is cut adrift by his stepmother and half-siblings to fend for himself on the streets and as a laborer and to survive on his own? After the days of agony and nights of loneliness end when his teen years also come to an end, does the boy simply go back to his real mother's family as if nothing happened and write the 'happy ending' to his book of life? Or does he continue to fight the shadows of demons as long as he lives? How does his earlier life shape and affect his later visions of life intellectually, politically, and personally? Would my life's records be radically different if my father had not died young and I had lived a very normal life which would likely be open to a clever, smart, and young boy like me in Korea?

The answer to all these questions may be in one word, providence, which means it is something beyond me. Of course, the story that I have told in this book covers only the first twenty years of my life. After I had a tearful meeting with my cousin, eventually to become my brother, I have so far lived five more decades, mostly in America and mostly as a professor. My days on the street and as a human engine are so far removed from the life that followed in America as a professor, almost like day and night. But are they that far apart from each other? My later life, perhaps wholly independent of my earlier life, perhaps a continuing dialog with my earlier life, is for another day.

Jon Huer
Professor Emeritus (meaning 'retired')
Sociology and Philosophy
University of Maryland University College

VIII. Books by Jon Huer

These are books that I have written that have gone into print. Along with my unpublished book manuscripts, often in quality superior to the published ones, these books of mine make up the totality my life as it has been lived in America. I am listing these books so that my story is complete, at least in this particular narrative. It's been a fulfilling life, mostly in quixotic pursuit of justice and equality, and what's more gratifying than being able to pursue one's own childhood dreams and fantasies? These books of mine, actually read by few, known to even fewer, and mostly unpopular, are my lifelong defense of America as the 'Shining City on the Hill,' a splendid beacon to the world that yearns for justice and equality—that comes closest to my intellectual dreams and utopian fantasies. Yes, even if your critique of America for having fallen short of such ideals risks hostility from your own professional colleagues and indifference from the reading public.

Above all, these books are my testimonials on the wonderful powers of providence, in whose benevolent shadow I have taken the long journey from the orphanage in the City of Glory to the Shining City on the Hill, which is perilously close to being neither shiny nor splendidly perched on the hill.

JAPAN'S QUIET CIRCLE (forthcoming 2020, English and Japanese versions, compares the two societies, Japan and the U.S.)

DONALD TRUMP, MADE IN THE U.S.A (2017, is about how white America created Trump)

LABOR AVOIDANCE: THE ORIGINS OF INHUMANITY (2015, answers the question: why is humanity so nasty to each other?)

CALL FROM THE CAVE: OUR CRUEL NATURE AND THE QUEST FOR POWER (2013, is about power, Hitler, and capitalism)

AUSCHWITZ, U.S.A (2010, is about the Holocaust and also analyzes Nazism and industrial efficiency in capitalism)

AMERICAN PARADISE *(2010, Arabic language edition 2018, describes America as a Fool's Paradise)*

THE GREEN PALMERS (Fiction 2007, a Stephen King-esque tale of evil and greed)

THE POST-HUMAN SOCIETY (2004, is about American society with its humanity gone)

THE WAGES OF SIN (1991, describes America's capitalism against Humanity)

TENURE FOR SOCRATES (1991, is about corruption in higher education)

THE GREAT ART HOAX (1990, is about art forgery and fakery and art as commercial product)

THE FALLACIES OF SOCIAL SCIENCE (1990, argues that so-called 'social science' is a fraud)

MARCHING ORDERS (1989, describes how South Korea marched to economic development and fame)

ART, BEAUTY, AND PORNOGRAPHY (1987, is a book about art, beauty, and pornography and how they relate or do not relate to one another)

IDEOLOGY AND SOCIAL CHARACTER (1978, is an exercise in sociological imagination)

SOCIETY AND SOCIAL SCIENCE (1978, another early exercise in sociological imagination)

THE DEAD END (1977, is my magnum opus, a prophecy about America's 'national death wish,' and is described as 'important and often brilliant' by TIME Magazine's Lance Morrow)

(End of *The Story of a Boy Favored by Providence*,
By Jon Huer)